CGP

GCSE WJEC B Religious Studies
Religion and Life Issues
(Unit 1)
The Revision Guide

Want to hear the **bad news**? There's an awful lot of heavy-going
stuff they expect you to learn for GCSE Religious Studies.

Want to hear the **good news**? Good old CGP have got it all covered!
We've produced this brilliant book, with all the key concepts explained
in clear, simple English so you can understand it — and remember it.

And then, in the spirit of going the extra mile, we've put in
a smattering of not-so-serious bits to try and make the
whole experience at least partly entertaining for you.

We've done all we can — the rest is up to you.

What CGP is all about

Our sole aim here at CGP is to produce the highest quality
books — carefully written, immaculately presented and
dangerously close to being funny.

Then we work our socks off to get them out to you
~~...~~

Contents

Topic Four — Our World

Guide to Symbols

This book covers Religion and Life Issues in the context of **Christianity** (including
Roman Catholic Christianity), **Islam** and **Judaism**.
The clouds in the corners of the pages tell you whether the page covers:

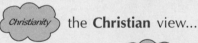 the **Christian** view...

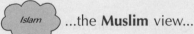 ...the **Muslim** view...

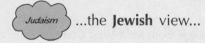 ...the **Jewish** view...

 ... or general views that **everyone** doing the
Religion and Life Issues unit needs to learn.

Bible / Qur'an References

References from the Bible always go in the order: **Book Chapter:Verse(s)**.
So whenever you see something like: **Mark 3:5-6**, it means it's from the
book of Mark, Chapter 3, Verses 5-6.

Similarly, references from the Qur'an are shown with the **Surah (Chapter)**
followed by the **Ayat (Verse)**.

Published by CGP

Editors:
Sharon Keeley, Andy Park, Rachael Powers, Julie Wakeling

Contributors:
Jill Hudson, Paul D. Smith

ISBN: 978 1 84762 304 1

With thanks to Mary Falkner and Karen Gascoigne for the proofreading.
With thanks to Laura Phillips for the copyright research.

Quotation on page 11 taken from the Catechism of the Catholic Church

Biblical quotations taken from the HOLY BIBLE, NEW INTERNATIONAL VERSION
Copyright © 1973, 1978, 1984 by International Bible Society
All rights reserved.
"NIV" is a registered trademark of the International Bible Society.
UK trademark number 1448790

Holy Qur'an quotations taken from the Holy Qur'an, Sahih International Version
www.quran.com

Hadith quotations taken from MSA West Compendium of Muslim Texts
www.msawest.net/islam

Photograph on page 10 reproduced by permission of Rex Features.

Every effort has been made to locate copyright holders and obtain permission to reproduce sources. For those sources where it has been difficult to trace the originator of the work, we would be grateful for information. If any copyright holder would like us to make an amendment to the acknowledgements, please notify us and we will gladly update the book at the next reprint. Thank you.

Groovy website: www.cgpbooks.co.uk

Jolly bits of clipart from CorelDRAW®
Printed by Elanders Ltd, Newcastle upon Tyne

Based on the classic CGP style created by Richard Parsons.

Love and Commitment

Christianity, Judaism, & Islam

This section is all about the <u>relationships</u> people have with <u>God</u> and with <u>each other</u>. We'll get started on a <u>cheery note</u> — the meaning of <u>love</u>...

Christians Believe Love is about Commitment...

LOVE

1) Christians use the word '<u>love</u>' to describe the immense and unconditional <u>kindness</u> and <u>affection</u> that <u>God</u> shows towards the <u>world</u> and to <u>mankind</u>.
2) It also describes the way <u>Christians</u> are supposed to <u>feel</u> towards <u>God</u>.
3) Christians also believe that we should <u>love each other</u> — as much as we <u>love ourselves</u>.

This idea of love isn't the same as the romantic meaning, which tends to mean having strong feelings for someone and fancying them.

"'Love the Lord your God with all your heart and with all your soul and with all your mind.' This is the first and greatest commandment. And the second is like it: 'Love your neighbour as yourself.'" Matthew 22:37-39

COMMITMENT

Why do I always get the ginger, slipper-wearing neighbour?

1) When you <u>commit</u> to something, you <u>promise</u> to do something. Commitments usually <u>stop</u> you from being able to freely do whatever you please.
2) Christians believe that they should <u>commit</u> their lives to God and <u>trust</u> him to <u>guide</u> them.
3) <u>Marriage</u> also requires <u>commitment</u>. The Bible says that a couple should commit to each other until they're <u>separated</u> by <u>death</u>.

...and also Responsibility

1) The Bible says Christians are <u>responsible</u> for <u>looking after</u> their <u>families</u> and the <u>people</u> that they <u>love</u>.
2) Christians are also expected to show <u>kindness</u> to people and <u>care for</u> them even if they <u>don't know</u> them. There are lots of examples of this in the Bible, such as the story of the <u>Good Samaritan</u> (Luke 10:30-37). It's about a man who stops to help someone who's been attacked by robbers. At the end of the story, Jesus tells his followers "Go and do likewise."

"If anyone does not provide for his relatives, and especially for his immediate family, he has denied the faith and is worse than an unbeliever." 1 Timothy 5:8

Jews are Told to Love Each Other and God

1) Like Christians, Jews believe that it's important to '<u>love your neighbour</u>', and also to <u>love God</u>.
2) The Torah says that <u>men</u> should spend their <u>whole life</u> with a <u>wife</u> they <u>love</u>.
3) It also says that Jews have <u>duties</u> (called <u>mitzvot</u> or '<u>commands</u>'), which they must fulfil. These include <u>learning</u>, <u>teaching</u> and <u>helping the poor</u>.

"Love the LORD your God with all your heart and with all your soul and with all your strength." Deuteronomy 6:5

The Qur'an talks about Love and Duty

1) Most <u>Muslims</u> believe that it's their <u>responsibility</u> to <u>obey Allah</u>. The word '<u>Islam</u>' literally means '<u>submission</u>' or '<u>obedience</u>' to Allah.
2) The Qur'an says lots about the <u>commitments</u> and <u>responsibilities to others</u> that Muslims have. For example, they have a responsibility to <u>care for</u> their <u>children</u>, be <u>kind</u> to their <u>parents</u> and to the <u>poor</u> and to <u>look after</u> <u>orphans</u>. Muslims are also committed to <u>worshipping only Allah</u>.
3) The Qur'an also says that Allah created man and woman so that they would feel <u>love</u> and <u>kindness</u> towards one another. It says that Allah <u>wanted</u> men and women to <u>get married</u>.

"The one who looks after a widow or a poor person is like a Mujahid (warrior) who fights for Allah's Cause, or like him who performs prayers all the night and fasts all the day." Prophet Muhammad (Sahih Bukhari)

Love matters more than anything — even exams...

You might want to try <u>revising anyway</u> though — I wouldn't fancy my chances at trying to fob off examiners with that excuse. The key thing to remember from this page is that, as far as religion goes, love isn't about <u>hearts</u>, <u>flowers</u>, <u>hot dates</u> at the cinema and stuff, it's a <u>responsibility</u> that we have to <u>others</u>, including <u>God</u>.

> Christianity, Judaism, Islam

Sexual Relationships

Christianity, Islam and Judaism have all formulated laws concerned with <u>sex</u>. But this doesn't mean that religious people think there is anything <u>wrong</u> or <u>dirty</u> about having sex — quite the <u>opposite</u>.

Christianity, Islam and Judaism have a Lot in Common...

The three faiths have a lot in common when it comes to <u>sex</u>.

1) <u>Traditionally</u> all three religions teach that sex is a <u>gift from God</u>, but that the only right context for it is within <u>marriage</u>.

2) Nowadays you find <u>liberal</u> Christians, Jews and Muslims who'll tell you that this belief is outdated.

> They might argue that when the <u>scriptures</u> were written, contraception was <u>unreliable</u> and the danger of unwanted pregnancy very <u>great</u>. But modern methods mean this isn't the case today.
> Also, allowing sex before marriage gives young people a chance to <u>explore</u> their sexuality and channel their sexual urges. It's argued that <u>sexual frustration</u> is a bad reason to get married.

3) But 'Orthodox' members of all faiths say that certain <u>moral principles</u> never change, and that couples <u>should</u> stay 'chaste' until they're <u>married</u> — this means not having <u>pre-marital sex</u>. It's very important to most <u>Muslims</u> that people, especially girls, remain <u>virgins</u> until marriage.

4) The Christian Church teaches that the total giving of self in sex shouldn't be treated <u>casually</u> — self-control and sexual restraint are considered important. Christians are urged to keep sex within <u>marriage</u> for <u>positive</u> reasons more than <u>negative</u> ones — marriage is believed to give sex a <u>special</u> status.

5) <u>Promiscuity</u> (having many sexual partners) is seen as wrong in all three religions.

...but they're Not Identical

1) Judaism and Christianity are <u>monogamous</u> — <u>adultery</u> (extra marital sex between a married person and someone who isn't their husband or wife) is forbidden by the Commandments.

2) Islam permits, but doesn't encourage, <u>polygamy</u>. A man may have up to four wives, but only if he can support them and treat them equally.

> <u>Muhammad</u> actually had <u>eleven wives</u> during his lifetime — although not all at the same time.

3) Some Christians (e.g. monks) take vows of <u>celibacy</u> — they renounce sex and marriage. They feel it helps them concentrate on God. Islam and Judaism <u>don't</u> agree with this — they believe that having a family is more important.

Family is Important to Christians, Jews and Muslims

1) Over the last 30 years, it's become more popular (and socially acceptable) for couples to <u>cohabit</u> (i.e. live together) — either <u>instead</u> of getting married or as a '<u>trial marriage</u>' before doing it for real. (However, government statistics suggest that a marriage is more <u>likely</u> to break down if the couple <u>lived together</u> first.)

2) There's also been a growth of <u>single-parent</u> families and <u>re-constituted</u> families (where divorcees with children <u>remarry</u>, or find new partners).

> This is partly due to more children being born outside marriage, but it's also because more than 1 in 3 marriages now end in <u>divorce</u>.

3) Despite these changes, Christians, Jews and Muslims all still regard the family as of high importance...

Christianity

1) <u>Family life</u> is seen as very important by most Christians — it's believed to be better for a child to have a <u>father</u> and a <u>mother</u> present (ideally the child's <u>biological</u> parents), so that he or she grows up with one <u>role model</u> of each sex.

2) Ideally, a stable family can give a child a sense of <u>identity</u> and a feeling of <u>security</u>, teaching him or her how to <u>behave</u> in different social situations, and how to give and receive <u>love</u>.

Islam

Muslims believe that a stable family life teaches people to be <u>kind</u>, <u>considerate</u> and <u>affectionate</u> towards others, and that it's the <u>duty</u> of the <u>father</u> to raise his children as Muslims.

Judaism

Family life is also very important to Jews, as it's through the family that the Jewish <u>religion</u> and <u>customs</u> are passed on. Children take part in <u>Shabbat rituals</u> (the special meals and prayers of the day of rest) at home from an early age.

Cohabit — when two nuns share an outfit...

Christianity, Judaism and Islam all teach that you shouldn't have sex before you're <u>married</u> — after that, they're all for it. But some people think their attitude to sex before marriage isn't <u>relevant</u> in today's society.

Contraception

Hmmm... another <u>tricky topic</u>...

Contraception — Preventing a Pregnancy

1) <u>Contraception</u> (or <u>birth control</u>) is anything that aims to <u>prevent</u> a woman becoming <u>pregnant</u> (<u>conceiving</u>).

2) Contraception can be <u>temporary</u> (e.g. the contraceptive pill, condoms) or <u>permanent</u> (sterilisation).

3) The Roman Catholic Church believes that preventing conception is against '<u>natural law</u>' and that the use of any artificial contraception is a <u>grave sin</u>. Indeed, it teaches that humans have an obligation to 'be fruitful and multiply'. Many <u>individual</u> Roman Catholics disagree with this, especially because of recent concerns about AIDS. The Church does allow <u>natural family planning</u> though — by only having sex at the times during a woman's cycle when she's less fertile.

Be fruitful and multiply...

4) Other Christian Churches have different views on the matter. The <u>Anglican</u>, <u>Methodist</u> and <u>Presbyterian Churches</u> are in favour of contraception, suggesting that it lets parents plan their family in a <u>responsible</u> way. Ideally, it should be something the couple decide together.

5) Many Christians believe that contraception should be a question of <u>individual conscience</u>.

Islam Teaches that Life is a Sacred Gift from Allah

1) The Qur'an encourages <u>procreation</u> and Muslims believe that conception is the will of Allah. So although <u>contraception</u> isn't specifically mentioned in the Qur'an, it's often seen as unwelcome.

> "...He gives to whom He wills female [children], and He gives to whom He wills males ...and He renders whom He wills barren..." Qur'an 42:49-50

2) Most Muslims feel that it's the <u>right</u> of both husband and wife to try for children, so <u>both partners</u> must <u>agree</u> to any contraception.

3) Different Muslims have different views on contraception, e.g. in Iran, contraception for family planning is <u>actively encouraged</u>. But more <u>conservative</u> scholars and clerics have campaigned against contraception.

In most Muslim countries, contraception is permitted if:
i) there's a threat to the <u>mother's health</u>,
ii) it could help a woman who <u>already</u> has children,
iii) there is a greater than average chance of the child being born with <u>disabilities</u>,
iv) the family is too <u>poor</u> to raise a child.

4) Only 'reversible' methods are allowed, though — <u>permanent sterilisation</u> and <u>vasectomies</u> are frowned on.

Jews Generally see Contraception as Bad

1) Judaism <u>traditionally</u> teaches that a child is a <u>gift</u> from God, and contraception <u>interferes</u> with God's plans to bless couples with children.

2) Most Orthodox Jews only accept contraception if pregnancy could be physically or psychologically <u>harmful</u> to the mother or an <u>existing</u> child. The couple might discuss the most acceptable method with their rabbi.

3) Reform Jews are happier with the idea of contraception for <u>family planning</u> — leaving the decision of whether or not to use it to individual conscience. (Having said that, <u>not wanting</u> to have children isn't a good enough reason to use contraception for many Jews.)

4) Sex should be as <u>natural</u> as possible, though, so hormonal contraceptives like the <u>contraceptive pill</u> are generally preferred to barrier methods like <u>condoms</u>. But their use may be encouraged by some as a means of preventing the spread of **HIV** and other **STIs** (sexually transmitted infections).

Nothing's ever simple is it...

People <u>interpret</u> their religion's teachings in different ways, so it's difficult to give a <u>clear-cut overview</u> of what a religion teaches. These are very 'human' topics, and people are very different. But all these different opinions about various issues makes for plenty to say in the exam.

Christianity

Marriage in Christianity

Marriage — a pretty big thing in anyone's life. Including yours if you get a question about it in the Exam.

Courting is a Bit Like Dating

1) The **Bible** doesn't say anything about how to find someone to marry, because in biblical times **marriages** were **arranged**. However, modern Christians believe that everyone has the **right to choose** who they marry.

2) Many Christians find a partner by **courting** (dating). Couples **don't** usually have **sex** during the courtship period because sex before marriage is **forbidden** by God.

A Christian Wedding has Legal, Social and Religious Features

Most Christian weddings take place in **church**. The details will vary according to **tradition** and **denomination**, but all combine **legal**, **social** and **religious** features:

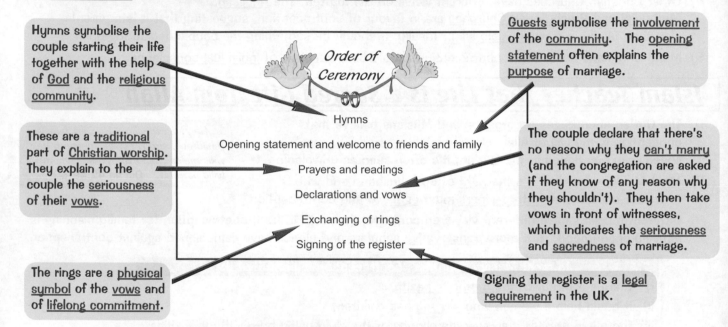

Hymns symbolise the couple starting their life together with the help of **God** and the **religious community**.

These are a **traditional** part of **Christian worship**. They explain to the couple the **seriousness** of their **vows**.

The rings are a **physical symbol** of the **vows** and of **lifelong commitment**.

Order of Ceremony

Hymns

Opening statement and welcome to friends and family

Prayers and readings

Declarations and vows

Exchanging of rings

Signing of the register

Guests symbolise the **involvement** of the **community**. The **opening statement** often explains the **purpose** of marriage.

The couple declare that there's no reason why they **can't marry** (and the congregation are asked if they know of any reason why they shouldn't). They then take vows in front of witnesses, which indicates the **seriousness** and **sacredness** of marriage.

Signing the register is a **legal requirement** in the UK.

A Roman Catholic wedding may also include **nuptial mass** (Holy Communion). In an Orthodox wedding, **crowns** are placed on the heads of the bride and groom.

Church Weddings are Less Popular than they Used to Be

1) In the past, most people married in church. However, now only around **1 in 3** weddings is in a **church**.

2) The number of weddings being held in **non-religious** venues, like hotels or castles, is **increasing**. Many people also choose to get married abroad, often somewhere hot and sunny.

You can't get married absolutely anywhere — the place has to have a special licence.

3) The ceremony will be a **civil ceremony** — it'll have absolutely no reference to religion.

4) Many Christians choose to marry in church so the wedding takes place '**in front of God**'.

5) The Church of England used to have **strict rules** about **which church** you could marry in — you had to have lived in the parish or worshipped there regularly. These rules were **relaxed** in 2008 to make it easier for couples to **choose** the church where they wanted to get married.

Don't let all this trouble and strife get you down...

The number of **marriages** in the UK is **falling**, but that doesn't make it a less **popular** topic with the **examiners**. Make sure you learn what happens during a Christian marriage **ceremony**, and what each bit **symbolises**. When that's done, try to think of some reasons **for** and **against** getting married in a church.

The Christian Church and Divorce

Christianity

Divorce used to be frowned upon by the Christian church — it's a bit more acceptable these days though...

Christians say Marriage Should be Forever

1) The Christian faith values marriage very <u>highly</u> — the joining of husband and wife in <u>holy matrimony</u> reflects the union of Jesus with his followers.

2) Jesus taught that marriage should be a <u>lifelong</u> union — marriage is seen as a <u>covenant</u> or <u>contract</u> between two people, involving <u>commitment</u> and <u>responsibility</u>. Christianity teaches that the purpose of marriage is for two people to offer mutual support and have children.

> "...a man will leave his father and mother and be united to his wife, and they will become one flesh." Genesis 2:24

The Bible gives Advice on Having a Successful Marriage

1) The Bible says that both people must be <u>faithful</u>. They mustn't have sex with anyone else (which would be <u>adultery</u>).

> "You shall not commit adultery." Exodus 20:14

2) It also says that marriage involves <u>submission</u> (devoting your life to the other person).

3) Many Christians believe that it's best to marry <u>another Christian</u>, or you'll be pulling in opposite directions.

Yokes were used to attach two working animals together.

> "Do not be yoked together with unbelievers." 2 Corinthians 6:14

> In Ephesians 5:21-33, wives are encouraged to <u>submit</u> to their husbands, and husbands to <u>love</u> their wives, laying down their lives for them as Christ laid down his.

Christian Churches have Different Attitudes to Divorce

The <u>breakdown</u> of a marriage is seen by all Christians as a <u>tragedy</u>. However, not all Christians agree about whether divorce is <u>permissible</u>, or even <u>possible</u>:

> The <u>Roman Catholic Church</u> states that it is actually <u>impossible</u> to divorce. Marriage is a <u>sacrament</u> — God has made the couple into one flesh, and this cannot be undone. However, a marriage can be <u>annulled</u> — annulment means that it was never a <u>true</u> marriage in the first place. This can happen if:
>
> i) either partner did not <u>consent</u> to the marriage or didn't <u>understand</u> what marriage is about,
>
> ii) the couple didn't or couldn't have <u>sex</u>, or one partner <u>refused</u> to have children.

> <u>Nonconformist</u> Churches (e.g. Baptists and Methodists) will generally remarry divorcees, but an <u>individual minister</u> can refuse to do so if this goes against his or her own conscience.

> The <u>Church of England</u> says that divorce is <u>acceptable</u>, but that divorced people can only remarry <u>in church</u> if they can find a minister willing to marry them. This doesn't satisfy every member of the Church of England.

1) The Bible talks a lot about <u>reconciliation</u>. Reconciliation is when <u>people</u> who <u>no longer get on</u> and are <u>in conflict</u> agree to <u>work through</u> their <u>problems</u>.

2) <u>Marriage counselling</u> can help a couple overcome conflict. The couple <u>talk through</u> their <u>problems</u> with a <u>professional counsellor</u> who listens and helps them find solutions. Some marriage counselling services, like Marriage Care, are <u>Christian</u> organisations.

Jesus talked about Divorce in the Gospels

Christians have a range of attitudes to divorce — maybe because Jesus was <u>anti-divorce</u>, but <u>pro-forgiveness</u>.

(1) *In Mark 10:2-12 Jesus says that Moses allowed divorce because of people's 'hardness of heart'. But he says that at the Creation of mankind marriages were meant to last for life, and if a divorcee remarries it's the same as adultery.*

(2) *Matthew 5:31-32 and 19:8-9 say the same thing — except that divorce is permitted to someone whose partner has already been unfaithful.*

(3) *In John 8:1-11, Jesus freely forgives a woman caught in the act of adultery. But he tells her, 'Go now and leave your life of sin'.*

Yes, dear...

Allegedly, those are the two most <u>important words</u> in a happy marriage. They're not actually mentioned in the Bible, but they are kind of implied in the stuff about <u>patience</u> and <u>forgiveness</u>. My personal tip for success would be to always let the lady have the <u>biggest wardrobe</u> and the <u>last chocolate</u> in the box...

Marriage and Divorce: Islam

Marriage is very important in Islam. Muslims are advised to marry, and Muhammad himself was married.

Marriage is Recommended for Three Reasons

1) Marriage provides companionship.

2) Marriage provides a secure environment for having children (procreation) and bringing them up as practising Muslims.

3) The sexual instinct is very strong and needs to be carefully channelled.

"...He created for you from yourselves mates that you may find tranquillity in them; and He placed between you affection and mercy..." Qur'an 30:21

"Whoever among you can marry, should marry, because it helps him lower his gaze and guard his modesty..." Prophet Muhammad (Sahih Bukhari)

Choosing a Partner is often your Parents' Responsibility

Practising Muslims generally want their children to marry other Muslims. Islam affects a Muslim's whole life, and being married to a non-Muslim could create tension, especially with bringing up children.

1) Most Muslims believe it's unwise for young men and women to mix freely, and 'dating' is discouraged or even forbidden.

2) In most Muslim communities, parents search for suitable partners for their children — i.e. Muslims often have 'arranged marriages'.

3) However, as marriage is a contract, both partners must consent to it.

4) Parents also have a responsibility to help if the marriage goes wrong.

The Marriage Ceremony — Customs Vary

The marriage ceremony is different in different Islamic cultures, but there's always a religious ceremony (witnessed by Allah) and a public one (witnessed by the community). They usually go like this...

1) A nikah (contract) is drawn up in advance by the families of the bride and groom, and a mahr (dowry) paid by the groom to the bride.

2) The bride doesn't have to be present — she can send two witnesses in her place.

3) An imam (leader of prayers) is often present (though this isn't compulsory).

4) Vows are exchanged, and a marriage declaration is made by each partner. There may be readings from the Qur'an or a khutbah (speech).

5) There will be a big feast afterwards, though the men and women may enjoy this separately.

6) The marriage ceremony can take place anywhere, although it's usually in a mosque or in the bride or groom's home.

If the venue is in the UK, but isn't registered, the religious ceremony must be followed by a registry office ceremony, so that the marriage will be recognised by the law.

Divorce is the Last Resort

1) Divorce is permitted, but only as a very last resort. If things aren't going well, an arbiter from each family should be appointed to try to sort things out.

2) Muslims see reconciliation as particularly important when the couple have children.

3) But, in Islam, marriage is a contract and like any other contract it can be ended.

"Of all the lawful acts the most detestable to Allah is divorce." Prophet Muhammad (Sunan Abu Dawud)

4) When the man says 'I divorce you' three times, the marriage is said to be over. However, there's often a period of three months after the first of these declarations. This allows time for reflection, and also to ensure that the woman is not pregnant.

This kind of divorce isn't legal in the UK, as Islamic law isn't part of the British legal system.

5) A woman can divorce a man in this way (divorce 'by talaq') if it was written into her marriage contract. Otherwise she has to apply to a Shari'ah court (a Muslim religious court) for a divorce 'by khul'.

6) After divorce, both men and women are free to remarry.

But I never said I wanted to study a foreign language...

Yep — quite a few Arabic words on this page. Marriage in Islam isn't a sacrament like in Christianity, it's a contract, with rights and obligations for both the bride and groom. But it's still considered pretty important.

Marriage and Divorce: Judaism

Traditionally all Jews have been <u>expected</u> to marry and have at least two children — a boy and a girl if possible.

Marriage Matters in Judaism

1) To Jews, marriage is an <u>emotional</u>, <u>intellectual</u> and <u>spiritual</u> union. It is seen as the proper context for <u>sex</u> (seen as natural and God-given) and having children (<u>procreation</u>), but is also for <u>companionship</u>.

2) It's the Jewish custom for parents to arrange for their children to meet suitable partners. To help with this it was common to use a 'shadchan', or <u>matchmaker</u> (and it still is among the ultra-Orthodox).

> Nowadays there are shadchan services available via the <u>Internet</u>.

3) Although 40% of UK Jews 'marry out' (i.e. marry non-Jews), those who take their religion seriously find this <u>worrying</u> — children of 'mixed marriages' are less likely to be brought up as <u>observant</u> Jews. Some Jews see this as a threat to Judaism's survival, and even a 'posthumous victory to Hitler'.

Kiddushin is the First Part of the Marriage Ceremony

'<u>Kiddushin</u>' is the first part of the marriage ceremony, and is usually translated as 'betrothal'. The word comes from a root meaning <u>sanctified</u>, which reflects the <u>holiness</u> of marriage.

Different Jewish communities celebrate marriage in different ways, but there are some <u>common features</u>.

1) The ceremony takes place beneath a <u>chuppah</u>, a wedding <u>canopy</u> — this is a piece of cloth supported by four poles. It is thought the cloth represents <u>privacy</u>, and the open sides <u>hospitality</u>.

2) Usually, the bride will <u>circle</u> the groom <u>seven times</u>.

3) The groom gives the bride a <u>ring</u> and makes the <u>betrothal declaration</u>: '*Behold you are consecrated to me with this ring according to the laws of Moses and Israel.*' This <u>completes</u> the kiddushin.

4) The <u>ketubah</u> (marriage contract) is read out and then <u>signed</u>. The traditional ketubah sets out the woman's right to be <u>cared for</u> by her husband and her entitlements in the event of divorce (a bit like a modern prenuptial agreement). Reform Jews have rewritten the ketubah to be a <u>mutual statement</u> of love and commitment, more like Christian marriage vows.

5) The <u>sheva brachot</u> or <u>seven blessings</u> are said over wine — normally by the rabbi. ← *The wine symbolises joy.*

6) The groom <u>breaks</u> a glass with his foot in memory of the destruction of the <u>Temple</u> in Jerusalem by the Romans in 70 CE. It's said that there can never be complete joy for the Jewish people until the Temple is restored — this is why it's remembered.

7) After the service there will be a festive meal and dancing, and shouts of 'mazel tov!' (good luck, best wishes). Among some Orthodox Jews, the men and women dance <u>separately</u>.

Divorce is a Last Resort

1) Judaism accepts that some marriages don't work out, and that it's better for a couple to divorce than to stay together in bitterness. But divorce is a very <u>last resort</u> after all attempts at <u>reconciliation</u> have failed.

2) Traditionally, a woman cannot <u>initiate</u> divorce, but a divorce does require the wife's <u>consent</u>.

3) In Reform synagogues, if the husband will not grant his wife a certificate of divorce (a 'Get') the <u>Bet Din</u> (Jewish court) can do so, freeing her to remarry.

4) In Orthodox synagogues, women who want a divorce but whose husbands will not grant one (or who aren't around to grant one) are known as '<u>agunot</u>' — chained women.

5) After the divorce, there are <u>no restrictions</u> on whether the man or woman may remarry.

Go on, learn it all — and I'll give you a Scooby-snack...

Rrrokay... Christian, Jewish and Muslim teachings about marriage and morality <u>have a lot in common</u>. It isn't so surprising — all three religions share the same <u>Near Eastern background</u>. Enjoy these few <u>happy</u> pages (apart from the divorce bits, that is) while you can — it doesn't stay like this through the whole book.

8

Same Sex Relationships

Another tricky topic — good job it's the last page in this section...

Homosexuality — Scriptures say it's Wrong

Homosexuality means being attracted to members of the same sex.

1) Homosexuality is seen in other species, and many non-religious people see it as a <u>natural alternative</u> to heterosexuality.

2) But the scriptures of all three religions <u>seem</u> to say that homosexual sex is <u>wrong</u> — although the relevant passages are interpreted <u>differently</u> by some people.

3) Some (including some priests) argue that the scriptures were written against a very different <u>cultural background</u> from ours, so we can't apply their standards today.

4) Christianity no longer <u>condemns</u> homosexuality, but it isn't seen as the <u>ideal</u> and many still view homosexual <u>sex</u> as a sin. So many religious gays opt for <u>celibacy</u> (they don't have sexual relationships).

> "Because of this, God gave them over to shameful lusts. Even their women exchanged natural relations for unnatural ones. In the same way the men also abandoned natural relations with women and were inflamed with lust for one another. Men committed indecent acts with other men, and received in themselves the due penalty for their perversion."
> Romans 1:26-27

Orthodox and Reform Jews have Different Views

1) Traditionally, Jewish people believed that <u>homosexuality</u> was <u>wrong</u>.

2) Many <u>Orthodox</u> Jews think that being a homosexual is <u>unnatural</u>, although it's <u>not forbidden</u>. People who are attracted to people of the same sex are expected to remain <u>celibate</u>.

3) <u>Reform</u> Jews don't usually condemn homosexuality and even allow <u>commitment ceremonies</u> for homosexuals — these can take place in a synagogue. They also allow homosexuals to become <u>rabbis</u>.

> "'Do not lie with a man as one lies with a woman; that is detestable."
> Leviticus 18:22

The Qur'an Seems to Say that Homosexuality is Wrong

1) Many Muslims believe that the <u>story</u> of the <u>people of Lot</u> in the <u>Qur'an</u> shows that <u>homosexuality</u> is <u>not permitted</u> in Islam. The story says that the people of Lot were <u>destroyed</u> by Allah's anger because they committed <u>homosexual acts</u>.

2) Homosexuality is strictly <u>forbidden</u> by Islamic Shari'ah law, so in many <u>Muslim</u> countries it's still <u>illegal</u>. In some countries, e.g. Iran and Saudi Arabia, homosexual acts between men carry the <u>death penalty</u>.

3) As with other religions though, some <u>moderate Muslims</u> believe that the Qur'an's views on homosexuality cannot be applied to <u>modern society</u>.

Civil Partnerships have been Legal Since 2005

1) <u>Civil partnerships</u> became <u>legal</u> in the UK in <u>December 2005</u>. They give homosexual couples the same <u>rights</u> as <u>married couples</u> concerning things like custody of children and shared finances.

2) A civil partnership <u>ceremony</u> takes place in a <u>register office</u> or <u>private venue</u>, such as a hotel, and is performed by a <u>registrar</u>.

3) The Church of England <u>doesn't allow</u> same-sex partnerships to be <u>blessed</u> in a <u>church</u>. However, there have been <u>some cases</u> where vicars have <u>gone against</u> this <u>rule</u> and blessed the unions of homosexual couples anyway.

Uncivil partnership

Oranges are not the only fruit, but that's all you're allowed to eat, apparently...

Oooh, here we go again... courting controversy. Whatever you think about this stuff yourself, <u>you still need to know what the religions teach</u>. Then you can agree or disagree with them all you like — it's up to you...

Practice Questions

Ding dong, ding dong, ding dong, ding dong... ah, don't you just love weddings. But as with most Ethics topics, it's not all champagne and roses. All three religions teach that marriage involves commitment and faithfulness, and that it's something that has to be <u>worked</u> at...

Speaking of which, it's about time you got to work on some practice questions. Have a go at answering them all. If there are any you struggle with, go back and have another look at the section. Then try the questions again until you can do them all.
(Have a look at the 'Do Well in Your Exam' and 'Glossary' pages at the back of the book for extra help.)

1) Explain what religious believers mean by:
   a) love.
   b) chastity.
   c) cohabitation.
   d) commitment.
   e) reconciliation.
   f) adultery.

Every question in the exam starts by asking you to explain what a key term means to religious believers. If you don't <u>learn</u> these ideas (and they're all in the <u>glossary</u>), you're throwing away an easy 2 marks.

2) Explain how having a religious faith may influence a couple deciding whether:
   a) to marry rather than cohabit.
   b) to get married in a castle.
   c) to have sex before marriage.
   d) to get divorced.

These are pretty big questions for the couples, but they're only worth 4 marks for you in the exam. Explain a few religious ideas about the issue, but don't waffle on and on. You don't have to refer to specific religions, but make sure you use key terms correctly.

3) Give <u>two</u> reasons why a religious believer might agree or disagree with each of these statements:
   a) "Religion can help keep a family together."
   b) "Getting a divorce is better than living in an unhappy marriage."
   c) "Homosexuality is wrong."

These questions are for 4 marks each too. You need to give two viewpoints and explain the reasons behind each of them. Make sure you include some religious teachings.

4) Explain, from <u>two</u> different religious traditions:
   a) the teachings about love.
   b) the important features of a wedding ceremony.
   c) the teachings about contraception.

These questions are for 6 marks each. Write down some religious ideas or practices, and make sure you explain the reasons behind them.

5) Say whether you agree with each of these statements. Give reasons for your answer, showing that you have thought of more than one point of view. You must refer to religious beliefs.
   a) "It is wrong to have sex before marriage."
   b) "It is up to the couple to decide whether to use contraception. It is nothing to do with religion."
   c) "Divorced people should never be allowed to remarry."

These are the 8-mark biggies. Whether you agree with the statement or not, make sure you back up your view with religious or moral reasons. Then put just as much effort into a explaining the reasons for having a different viewpoint.

Topic One — Relationships

Social Justice and Responsibility

General

The stuff on this page is important for the smooth running of society. And religions have a view on it too...

Identity — Who You Are

1) Your identity is what makes you <u>you</u>. It's how you see yourself, as well as how other people see you.

2) It's made up of <u>basic stuff</u> like your name, age, gender and appearance, as well as '<u>deeper</u>' stuff such as your beliefs and attitudes.

3) Your identity is influenced by your <u>religion</u> and your <u>ethnic background</u>. People from the same religion or ethnic background will have some things <u>in common</u> — but they'll also <u>differ</u> in a lot of ways.

Social Responsibility is all about How We Treat Each Other

There are <u>three tricky concepts</u> that crop up time and again in this section:

1) <u>Social responsibility</u> is the idea that we should consider the <u>impact</u> our <u>actions</u> have on the <u>rest of society</u>, not just the impact they have on our own lives — it's basically about not being selfish.

2) <u>Social justice</u> is when <u>everyone</u> in society is <u>treated fairly</u> and their <u>basic human needs</u> are <u>satisfied</u>, e.g. they have somewhere to live, enough food to eat, etc. <u>Religions</u> all have a view on social responsibility and justice. They teach that we're all <u>accountable</u> for our actions, and that we should treat others as we'd want to be treated — the old "<u>love your neighbour</u>" thing.

Despite Ben's squawking about human dignity the bow remained.

3) <u>Human dignity</u> is the idea that <u>human life</u> is <u>valuable</u>, and every person has the right to be treated with <u>respect</u> — regardless of religion, race or social class, i.e. whatever their identity. All religions teach this. Human dignity is also linked to all people having <u>basic rights</u>, e.g. the right to freedom.

> In the UK, the freedom to practise any religion you choose (including no religion at all) is a legal <u>right</u>.

Authority Influences What People Do

People let authority <u>guide their actions</u>. There are lots of different types of authority — here's some examples:

1) The <u>law</u> (along with people who enforce it, such as the police and magistrates).

2) A person's own <u>conscience</u> — that little moral voice inside your head.

3) <u>Religious leaders</u>, e.g. the Pope has a massive influence over Catholics.

4) <u>Sacred texts</u>, such as the Bible and the Qur'an.

5) The <u>media</u> has a massive influence on people's attitudes too...

> The Pope is considered to be infallible on matters of faith and morals (i.e. he can't make a mistake).
>
> Mimmo Chianura/Rex Features

The Media is Becoming More Important

1) The influence of the media (newspapers, TV, internet etc.) has become <u>massive</u> in recent years — especially with satellite and digital television, and, of course, the Internet. You can't avoid the media.

2) At the same time, <u>church attendances</u> have been falling dramatically — many people would say that the media is now a <u>bigger authority</u> than the Church.

3) The media can affect people's attitudes — for better or worse...

- <u>Newspapers</u> carry a range of stories, e.g. coverage of wars, terrorism, racist crime and refugees, as well as a variety of other moral issues. This is where many people go to find out the 'truth'. But some people worry about how the ideas of the people who <u>own</u> or <u>write for</u> newspapers affect their content. This might include <u>political bias</u> or <u>xenophobia</u> (i.e. hatred of foreigners). You might find completely different versions of the same story in 'The Daily Telegraph', 'The Sun', and 'The Daily Mail'.

- The media <u>can</u> educate people about <u>different faiths</u> — both through serious documentaries and through soaps and films. However, misrepresentation can give a religion a '<u>bad name</u>'.

I have a problem with ~~authourity, authoraty~~ — I can't spell it...

In an ideal world there'd be no exams. Everyone would just believe in your brilliance and you wouldn't have to prove you knew a thing. But alas, it's <u>not</u> an ideal world, so there's nowt to do but get learning.

Wealth — Christianity

Wealth is basically <u>money and possessions</u>. Wealth is a big issue because it's not very evenly distributed in society — some people are rolling in it, whereas other people are left struggling in poverty. All religions have teachings about wealth — and here are Christianity's...

It's What You Do With Your Money that Counts

1) The Bible <u>doesn't say</u> that being <u>wealthy</u> is <u>wrong</u>. There are people in the Bible who are both wealthy and faithful to God. Of course, Christians believe you should only earn money in <u>moral ways</u> that don't hurt anyone, e.g. not through drug dealing. They often disapprove of <u>gambling</u> too (especially Methodists).

2) There are many passages in the Bible that suggest that Christians should <u>use</u> their <u>money</u> for <u>charity</u> and to show <u>compassion</u> and <u>care for other people</u>.

> *"The man with two tunics should share with him who has none, and the one who has food should do the same."* Luke 3:11

> *"I was hungry and you gave me something to eat, I was thirsty and you gave me something to drink... whatever you did for one of the least of these brothers of mine, you did for me."* Matthew 25:35-40

3) The <u>Story of the Rich Young Man</u> (Mark 10:17-31) warns that people find it <u>difficult</u> to <u>give away</u> their <u>money</u> to better serve God. He says *"It is easier for a camel to go through the eye of a needle than for a rich man to enter the kingdom of God."* — you can't serve <u>both</u> God and money.

Still looks pretty tricky to me...

The Sermon on the Mount says a lot about Money

The <u>Sermon on the Mount</u> is one of the most important summaries of Jesus' moral teaching found in the Gospels. It appears as a collection in Matthew 5:1 - 7:29, but much of the same material is also in <u>Luke</u>.

The Beatitudes (Matthew 5:3-12)

The sermon begins with a passage on true happiness (what it means to be 'blessed') — this is not to be found in wealth or pride, but in a simple, humble life, lived in obedience to God.

> "Blessed are the meek, for they will inherit the earth."

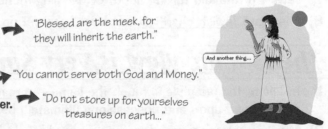

And another thing...

Christians and Money (Matthew 6:19-24)

It's impossible to love God and money equally. Also earthly riches are only temporary, whereas riches in heaven last forever.

> "You cannot serve both God and Money."

> "Do not store up for yourselves treasures on earth..."

Christians and Worry (Matthew 6:25-34)

Christians shouldn't worry about whether they'll have enough of the things they need — they should concentrate on loving God and trust him to provide them with clothes and enough to eat and drink.

> "But seek first his kingdom and his righteousness, and all these things will be given to you as well."

Christians have a Duty to Relieve Poverty

> *"Rich nations have a grave moral responsibility towards those which are unable to ensure the means of their development by themselves."* from the <u>Catechism</u> of the Roman Catholic Church: paragraph 2439

A number of Christian organisations exist to tackle poverty — both in the UK and on a global level. These include <u>Christian Aid</u> (see page 17) and <u>CAFOD</u>.

<u>Mother Teresa</u> is an example of a Christian who did a lot to fight against poverty:

> Mother Teresa was an Albanian Roman Catholic nun who devoted herself to the destitute and dying in Calcutta, India. She founded the Order of the Missionaries of Charity, whose nuns now work amongst the poor all over the world. She said that it isn't <u>what</u> you do for God that counts, but <u>how much love</u> you pour into it. She won the Nobel Peace Prize in 1979, and died in 1997 at the age of 87.

Money is the root of all evil — or maybe exams are...

The basic message here is very simple. It's OK for Christians to be wealthy, as long as they use their money to help the poor — some Christians will give a tithe, or ten percent of their income, to the Church or a charity.

Wealth — Judaism and Islam

Islam and Judaism have similar views on poverty. Both believe it's our duty to look after those less fortunate than ourselves, and both expect people to give some of their income to the poor and needy.

Judaism says, "Do not be hardhearted or tightfisted..."

1) This passage from Deuteronomy sums up Jewish teaching on poverty:

   "If there is a poor man among your brothers in any of the towns of the land that the LORD your God is giving you, do not be hardhearted or tightfisted toward your poor brother." Deuteronomy 15:7

2) Also, Maimonides said that the best way to give was "*to help a person help themselves so that they may become self-supporting*".

   Maimonides was an important Jewish Rabbi and philosopher.

3) There are two main ways of giving to charity — Tzedakah and Gemilut Hasadim:

   > TZEDAKAH: Tzedakah is financial aid — even the poorest in society are expected to contribute 10% of their wealth. All wealth belongs to God, and not giving to the poor deprives them of what they're owed.
   >
   > GEMILUT HASADIM: This refers to kind and compassionate actions towards those in need.

4) Many Jewish homes have collection boxes (called pushkes) in which money for charity can be placed. Children are encouraged to use these boxes — maybe donating some of their pocket money each week.

5) Although Judaism doesn't teach that everyone should try to be wealthy, it does suggest that extreme poverty will make others responsible for you. But the love of wealth may turn you from God — so you should neither seek nor shun wealth.

6) Unfairness and dishonesty in business are condemned — you're answerable to God for any wrongdoing.

7) Jews try to avoid talking about or handling money on the Sabbath (the day of rest).

8) There are Jewish charities that have been set up to help the poor — see page 17.

The Islamic View is Very Similar

1) In Islam, the principle is much the same — greed and waste are frowned upon and possessions ultimately belong to Allah.

   "Do not shut your money bag; otherwise Allah too will with-hold His blessings from you. Spend (in Allah's Cause) as much as you can afford." Prophet Muhammad (Sahih Bukhari)

2) Muslims are encouraged to act responsibly and help those in need.

3) Muslims believe that wealth must be earned through honest means — in ways permitted by the Qur'an. Gambling is forbidden, and moneylending is seen as immoral if those in debt are being exploited through the charging of interest. Some Islamic banks exist to get around this.

4) Again, there are two main ways to help the disadvantaged — Zakah and Sadaqah:

   > ZAKAH: This is one of the Five Pillars of Islam — 2.5% of your yearly savings should be given to the needy, no matter how rich or poor you are.
   >
   > SADAQAH: This is additional aid — maybe financial donations, or an act of compassion and love.

5) This Hadith sums up the importance of Zakah pretty clearly:

   "Whoever is made wealthy by Allah and does not pay the Zakah of his wealth, then on the Day of Resurrection his wealth will be made like a bald-headed poisonous male snake with two black spots over the eyes. The snake will encircle his neck and bite his cheeks and say, 'I am your wealth, I am your treasure.'" Prophet Muhammad (Sahih Bukhari)

6) There are Islamic charities, that help the poor globally — such as Islamic Relief and Muslim Aid (see p17).

It all sounds like good advice to me...

Both Islam and Judaism teach that we have a responsibility to our fellow man, and that we don't actually 'own' our wealth — it all belongs to God. And the more we have of it, the more generous we should be.

Prejudice and Equality

The world we live in is full of people from different <u>religious</u>, <u>racial</u> and <u>cultural</u> backgrounds.
And the way each religion deals with this is important, as it can help or hinder the building of <u>communities</u>.

Prejudice has Many Causes

It's worth being very clear about what a few words mean...

> **Equality** being <u>equal</u>, and being <u>treated equally</u>.
> **Prejudice** <u>judging</u> something or someone with no good reason, or without full knowledge of a situation.
> **Discrimination** <u>unjust treatment</u>, often resulting from prejudice.

1) Prejudice has many <u>causes</u>, and is often the product of <u>early influences</u>.
   It tends to be the result of <u>widely held</u> (yet <u>inaccurate</u>) beliefs of a particular community or family.

2) <u>Discrimination</u> comes in many forms... <u>Individuals</u> may discriminate by being <u>violent</u> and <u>abusive</u>.
   Whole <u>societies</u> may discriminate by passing <u>laws</u> which prevent certain people from doing certain things.

Racism is One Form of Prejudice

It's a sad fact that some people are prejudiced against anyone from a different <u>cultural</u> or <u>religious</u>
background, or simply because of the <u>colour</u> of their skin.

1) <u>Racial discrimination</u> has always been around. E.g. black people used to be used as slaves.
   But it still goes on. There have been many instances in the UK in recent years — usually as
   a result of <u>ignorance</u> or <u>misunderstanding</u>. At times these have culminated in <u>rioting</u> or <u>murder</u>.

2) Racism is often based on <u>stereotypes</u> — fixed and standardised images of
   groups of people, which can be used to promote <u>negative</u> thoughts and actions.

Sex Discrimination is Another

In the past, it was seen as a woman's role to take care of the <u>home</u> and raise <u>children</u>,
while the men went out to <u>work</u>. The man was the <u>head</u> of the household, and his wife
was expected to be <u>obedient</u>. After World War II, these attitudes started to change.
Things have come a <u>long way</u> since then, but there are still cases of disorimination,
e.g. sometimes people don't get jobs, purely because of their <u>gender</u>.

*Charles was a modern man — but
he just couldn't find where his
wife kept the lumps for the gravy.*

Is Equality Possible? — Well, Maybe...

1) <u>Laws</u> can be put in place to try to stop discrimination. For example:

> The <u>Race Relations Act</u> makes it <u>illegal</u> to discriminate
> on the grounds of race, colour or nationality, or to
> publish anything likely to <u>cause</u> racial hatred.

> The <u>Sex Discrimination Act</u> makes it
> <u>illegal</u> to discriminate against people
> on account of their <u>gender</u>.

2) Laws may stop people being openly discriminated against, but it's harder to change people's <u>attitudes</u>:

> People of different races and faiths often don't feel that they have much in common — even if they
> live in the same <u>community</u>. The Government is trying to promote the idea of '<u>Britishness</u>' as
> something that goes beyond <u>social divisions</u> to help with <u>community cohesion</u>.

> The <u>media</u> has an important role to play.
> Television and newspapers can <u>educate</u> — or
> help fuel <u>negative</u> stereotypes (see page 10).

> <u>Education</u> can help — Citizenship classes
> in school help teach about diversity.

3) <u>Positive discrimination</u> is when resources or jobs are set aside for groups that have been treated
   unfairly in the past — e.g. women or members of ethnic minorities. This can help people from these
   groups, but it can also cause <u>resentment</u> from others.

Community cohesion — you could always try superglue...

This is <u>difficult</u> and <u>emotive</u> stuff, but like all Religion and Life Issues topics, it's not supposed to be easy...

Christianity

Attitudes To Equality: Christianity

For Christians, the <u>Bible</u> has plenty to say on the subject of equality...

The Bible has Plenty of 'Anti-Prejudice' Stories

1) The idea of *'do to others what you would have them do to you'* (Matthew 7:12) is a fundamental part of Christian teaching (sometimes called the 'Golden Rule').

2) Generally Christians believe that everyone was created <u>equal</u> by God, and so they try to <u>avoid discrimination</u> and <u>promote equality</u>. They look to the example of Jesus, who told <u>stories</u> about equality, and acted true to his own teaching by <u>mixing</u> with a variety of people himself.

3) One of the most famous stories in the New Testament is the Parable of the <u>Good Samaritan</u> (Luke 10:25-37) where one man comes to the aid of another simply because he is <u>suffering</u>.

> ### The Parable of the Good Samaritan
> A man is beaten up and left half-dead by robbers. First a priest and then a Levite (the Levites were a Jewish priestly tribe) walking down the road see him, but carry on walking. But a Samaritan (considered an enemy by the Jews) bandages the man, puts him on his donkey, takes him to an inn and sees that he is looked after.

Quite right too.

4) And there are plenty of other verses preaching equal treatment for all:

"Do not deprive the alien or the fatherless of justice..." Deuteronomy 24:17

By the way, 'alien' means 'foreigner' here.

"...loose the chains of injustice and untie the cords of the yoke, to set the oppressed free... then your light will break forth like the dawn..." Isaiah 58:6-10

5) But although Christianity generally promotes <u>racial harmony</u> (people of all races living and working together peacefully), there have been occasions when this hasn't been the case...

Not <u>really</u> what we were after, guys...

> <u>Apartheid</u> was the system of racial segregation that existed in South Africa from 1948 to 1994. It began because the Dutch Reformed Church of South Africa (DRC) believed that God had <u>divided</u> mankind into different races and made <u>white people</u> superior.

Many People have Fought against Prejudice

There are many examples of <u>individual Christians</u> struggling against injustice — e.g.:

> <u>ARCHBISHOP DESMOND TUTU</u> and <u>BISHOP TREVOR HUDDLESTON</u> were active in the fight against apartheid in South Africa.

 <u>DR MARTIN LUTHER KING</u> was a baptist minister who dedicated his life to trying to change the way black people were treated in the USA. King was assassinated in 1968 aged only 39.

Sex Discrimination — Not So Clear

1) The Bible gives different messages about <u>sex discrimination</u>. In the New Testament, women are found among Jesus' followers and he treated them <u>equally</u> — remarkable for the time.

2) But this is taken from <u>St Paul</u>'s letter to his assistant <u>Timothy</u>:

> *"I do not permit a woman to teach or to have authority over a man; she must be silent. For Adam was formed first, then Eve... it was the woman who was deceived and became a sinner. But women will be saved through childbearing..."* 1 Timothy 2:12-15

3) Although in Galatians 3:28 St Paul writes, "There is neither... male nor female, for you are all one in Christ Jesus."

This shows that religious texts can often be interpreted in more than one way — and they're sometimes used to justify discrimination.

4) For <u>much</u> of the Church's history, women <u>haven't</u> been allowed to be ordained as <u>priests</u>. One of the reasons is that Jesus only called <u>men</u> to be Apostles. Over the last <u>50 years</u>, this has started to <u>change</u> — women can now be ordained as <u>ministers</u> in most Protestant denominations and as <u>Anglican priests</u>, but <u>not</u> as Roman Catholic or Orthodox priests.

The Good Samaritan — what a nice bloke...

This is a serious issue that often makes it into the <u>news</u>. And it's one that you might have experience of. But be careful not to just <u>rant</u> on in the exam — you need to refer to the religious teachings as well.

Attitudes To Equality: Judaism

Judaism

Like Christianity, <u>Judaism</u> teaches that God created people <u>equal</u>.

The Hebrew Bible Preaches Tolerance

<u>Racism</u> is disapproved of in Judaism. The Hebrew Bible (the Old Testament) has a lot to say on the matter.

1) The Book of Genesis suggests that all of humanity comes from the <u>same source</u> and is, therefore, <u>equal</u> before God. ➤

> "Adam named his wife Eve, because she would become the mother of all the living." Genesis 3:20

2) And here's a message of <u>tolerance</u> from Deuteronomy. ➤
(also see Deuteronomy 24:17 and Isaiah 58:6-10 on the previous page).

> "Do not abhor an Edomite, for he is your brother. Do not abhor an Egyptian, because you lived as an alien in his country." Deuteronomy 23:7

3) Deuteronomy 23 contains a discussion of who should be called 'the Lord's people'. It could be taken to mean that we should show <u>tolerance</u> for other nationalities. However, the same chapter does contain references to certain people or nations who should be <u>excluded</u>.

> *Again, this could be misused by someone to justify racism.*

4) The Jewish people are sometimes called the '<u>chosen people</u>'. This doesn't mean they think they're <u>better</u> than anyone else — simply that God gave them additional <u>responsibilities</u>.

5) The stories of <u>Ruth</u> and <u>Jonah</u> (both in the Hebrew Bible, i.e. the Old Testament) could also be used to promote <u>social</u> and <u>racial</u> harmony.

The Story of Jonah...

Jonah was told to preach to the people of Nineveh, who had <u>upset God</u>. When he preached God's message, the people of Nineveh were humble and repentant, which pleased God, and so God <u>spared</u> the city, <u>upsetting</u> Jonah. But God said he was right to spare the city, and that Jonah was wrong to be upset. The message is,
"If God can love and forgive, we should be able to live with others too."

> First I get thrown off the boat, then I get eaten by a big fish. This must be a Monday.

Before he got to Nineveh, Jonah was swallowed by a big fish and stayed there for 3 days.

> *And Isaiah 42:6 shows that God does not want the Jews to turn their backs on non-Jews, but to be "a light for the Gentiles".*

The Story of Ruth...

Naomi and her husband leave Judah because of a famine — they end up in <u>Moab</u>. Naomi's sons marry Moabite girls — but soon after, Naomi's husband and sons <u>die</u>. <u>Ruth</u> (one of Naomi's daughters-in-law) stays very <u>loyal</u> to her <u>Israelite mother-in-law</u>, and becomes devoted to God. Her bloodline eventually produces <u>King David</u>.
The message is, *"Good things happen to those who are nice to people from other lands."*

"Male and female he created them" — Genesis 1:27

1) The above passage is sometimes read as meaning that men and women are seen as <u>equals</u> before God, although <u>different</u>, and with different <u>responsibilities</u>. (God did create two different <u>sexes</u> after all, so he can't have wanted us all to be identical.)

2) Some people involved with the <u>feminist</u> movement (fighting for women's rights) argue that the expectation for women to become wives and mothers is <u>unfair</u>, and has <u>hindered</u> women's progress.

3) Judaism doesn't suggest that women should <u>not</u> be able to follow their chosen career. However, there is still a belief that motherhood is a <u>privilege</u>, and women should devote some of their life to it.

4) But there are definitely differences of opinion on this. <u>Orthodox Jews</u> aim to uphold many of the ancient Jewish <u>traditions</u>, and so would be more likely to suggest that women should remain at home as <u>mothers</u> and <u>wives</u>.

> There are also rules governing <u>SYNAGOGUE WORSHIP</u>. Usually ten <u>men</u> (called a minyan) are required for a service, and it is <u>men</u> who read from the Torah. Also, in Orthodox synagogues, men and women pray in <u>separate</u> areas.
>
> <u>Reform Jews</u> don't accept all these rules, however — women can form a minyan, and even become rabbis.

5) However, <u>Reform Jews</u> are willing to <u>interpret</u> traditional teachings so that they are, perhaps, more relevant to the <u>modern age</u>. For this reason they're less strict when it comes to the roles of men and women.

I don't believe the Jonah story — it all sounds a bit fishy...

Jews have suffered from a great deal of racism and persecution over the years. By far the most extreme form of social injustice was the <u>Holocaust</u> in World War II, when discrimination became <u>government policy</u>. It serves as a reminder to everyone of how much suffering can arise from racial hatred. It's bad. Really bad.

Islam

Attitudes To Equality: Islam

Islam is truly <u>international</u> — with followers from many countries, and many ethnic and cultural backgrounds.

Islam says People are Created Equal, but not Identical

1) Islam teaches that all people were created by Allah, and were created <u>equal</u> (although not the <u>same</u>). He intended humanity to be created with <u>differences</u>. But this just means we're all individuals. Hurrah.

> "And of His signs is the creation of the heavens and the earth and the diversity of your languages and your colours..." Qur'an 30:22

2) Muslims all over the world are united through the <u>ummah</u> — the community of Islam. The ummah consists of <u>all</u> Muslims, regardless of colour, nationality, tradition (i.e. Sunni or Shi'ite) and so on. This can help promote racial and social harmony, as no one is <u>excluded</u> or <u>discriminated</u> against (in theory).

Muslims are more likely to be subjected to <u>racially motivated</u> attacks, abuse and murder than their white neighbours in the UK.

As a result, a number of peaceful <u>pressure groups</u> have been established — some working within Muslim communities, others working with the Government or with other faith groups.

3) <u>Hajj</u> (pilgrimage to Makkah) especially demonstrates <u>equality</u>. Those on pilgrimage all wear simple white garments, showing that <u>everyone's</u> equal before Allah — wealth, status and colour don't matter.

4) The fact that <u>all</u> Muslims should <u>pray</u> five times a day at set times, and face Makkah whilst doing so, also demonstrates <u>unity</u> and <u>equality</u>. Men and women often pray <u>together</u> at home — however, they must pray in <u>separate groups</u> in the mosque.

The Qur'an teaches that Men and Women are Equal

1) Men and women have an <u>equal obligation</u> to Allah in terms of prayer, fasting, pilgrimage and charity. And <u>all</u> Muslims, male and female, are obliged to seek <u>education</u>:

> "Indeed, the Muslim men and Muslim women, the believing men and believing women, the obedient men and obedient women... the charitable men and charitable women, the fasting men and fasting women... and the men who remember Allah often and the women who do so — for them Allah has prepared forgiveness and a great reward." Qur'an 33:35

2) In the early days of Islam, there were many female <u>religious scholars</u>.

3) There are also some teachings that might be <u>interpreted</u> as meaning men are <u>superior</u>, e.g.

> "Men are in charge of women by [right of] what Allah has given one over the other and what they spend [for maintenance] from their wealth..." Qur'an 4:34

But these teachings are usually taken to mean that men and women just have different <u>roles</u> within the community or family — men are responsible for <u>providing</u> for the family, and women are responsible for the <u>home</u>.

WOMEN AND THE MOSQUE

<u>Women</u> aren't encouraged to attend the mosque for prayer, but the Prophet Muhammad did <u>permit</u> it. If they do go to the mosque, they must pray in a <u>separate group</u> — <u>behind</u> (or otherwise out of sight of) the men.

Women are not permitted to <u>lead</u> the prayers of men, but they may lead other women. This is agreed by <u>all</u> traditional schools of Islam, both Sunni and Shi'ite.

Muslim feminist <u>Asra Nomani</u> is leading a campaign to end segregation in the mosque, and allow woman-led <u>mixed-gender</u> prayers. In 2005, <u>Amina Wadud</u> led a mixed-gender prayer in New York. Their actions have been <u>condemned</u> by Muslim scholars as not following the teachings of Islam.

Equal but not the same — don't try that one in maths...

In Islam, a woman's <u>traditional</u> role has been to create a good homelife for the family, while the man went out to work and made sure the children were good Muslims. However, not all Muslims live in this traditional way. In some cultures there is almost complete equality between men and women.

Responding to Injustice

Christianity, Islam and Judaism agree that <u>all</u> human beings should be treated <u>fairly</u> and <u>humanely</u>, and there are organisations from <u>all three faiths</u> working to reduce injustice...

Some Religious Organisations Tackle Poverty

CHRISTIAN AID

Christian Aid was set up after World War II to help <u>refugees</u>. It now has over 40 member churches in the UK and Ireland, and works <u>globally</u> to relieve poverty. It raises money through <u>donations</u> and <u>collections</u>.

Most of Christian Aid's work is in <u>development</u>. Although they do contribute to emergency disaster relief, they believe the <u>best</u> way to help people is by '*helping them to help themselves*'. They set up projects in the Third World drawing on the skills of <u>local people</u>. This is seen as more dignified than receiving <u>hand-outs</u>.

Development projects set up by Christian Aid aim to help with problems such as poor <u>sanitation</u>, <u>education</u> and <u>healthcare</u>, as well as encouraging the use of <u>birth control</u>. The organisation also aims to change <u>government policy</u>, to help reduce the suffering of the world's poor, e.g. through Third World <u>debt relief</u>, and <u>fair-trade</u> products.

TZEDEK (JEWISH ACTION FOR A JUST WORLD)

Tzedek is a Jewish charity set up in the UK that works with poor people of all races and religions, '*providing direct support to small scale sustainable self-help development projects for the relief and elimination of poverty*'.

Their focus is on helping <u>local projects</u>, e.g. health and agriculture training schemes, that improve a community's ability to get itself <u>out of poverty</u> and achieve a <u>better standard of living</u>.

MUSLIM AID

Muslim Aid provides <u>disaster relief</u> and <u>development aid</u> around the world.

They aim to provide not only <u>initial emergency aid</u> after a war or natural disaster, but <u>ongoing help</u> to get people back on their feet. This help includes building <u>new permanent housing</u>, <u>sanitation</u> and <u>schools</u>, and offering <u>small interest-free loans</u> to help start up businesses.

Immigrants Often Face Difficulties

Over <u>100,000</u> people move to the UK every year — either looking for <u>work</u> or to find <u>refuge</u> from persecution (<u>asylum seekers</u>). And there are plenty of religious organisations out there to help them...

The Boaz Trust

A <u>Christian</u> organisation based in Greater Manchester, set up to help <u>failed asylum seekers</u>. These are people whose asylum applications have been turned down but who are too scared to go home. They aren't allowed to <u>work</u> in the UK and get <u>no</u> help from the Government, so they're entirely dependent on charity for food, accommodation and any <u>legal help</u> they might need for an appeal.

Islamic Aid

An international Muslim organisation dedicated to reducing <u>poverty</u> and <u>deprivation</u>. Their work in the UK centres on improving the lives of Muslim immigrants, e.g. by raising awareness of the problem of '<u>ghettos</u>' and tackling <u>unemployment</u> among UK Muslims.

The Jewish Council for Racial Equality (JCORE)

A Jewish organisation, based in the UK. They <u>campaign</u> for the rights of asylum seekers, <u>raise awareness</u> of the problems faced by immigrants and offer all sorts of <u>practical help</u>. For example, they have a '<u>refugee doctors project</u>' that gives information and practical help to trained immigrant doctors, to help them re-train to practise in the UK.

Bienvenue, Willkommen, Witajcie, Swaagatam, Huan yin...

The religions all preach justice for all. These charities are one way that they put their teachings into action.

Practice Questions

Can't we all just learn to get along? Well, no — you have to learn all the stuff in this section first.
This covers some pretty big issues — prejudice, discrimination, equality... and it's your job to pick your
way through this muddle that we call twenty-first century society.

Shall we begin...?

1) Explain what religious believers mean by:

   a) authority.

   b) human dignity.

   c) identity.

   d) social responsibility.

   e) social justice.

   f) Gemilut Hasadim. *(Judaism)*

   g) Tzedakah. *(Judaism)*

   h) Zakah. *(Islam)*

   i) Sadaqah. *(Islam)*

   To get the 2 marks for these questions you just have to <u>learn</u> what the key terms mean — it's that simple.

2) Explain how having a religious faith may:

   a) encourage someone to give to charity.

   b) encourage someone to join a protest against racism.

   c) support the view that we should be socially responsible.

   d) encourage someone to volunteer at a homeless shelter.

   "Explain" means you have to say <u>why</u>, not just <u>what</u> people believe. They're worth 4 marks each in the exam, so they're important.

3) Give <u>two</u> reasons why a religious believer might agree or disagree with each of these statements:

   a) "You earned your money, you should use it for whatever you want."

   b) "It is more important to help people in this country than to help foreigners."

   c) "Prejudice is always wrong."

   To get your 4 marks for these questions, you've got to explain two viewpoints — and remember to include religious teachings as well as moral ideas.

4) Explain, from <u>two</u> different religious traditions:

   a) the teachings about wealth.

   b) the teachings about equality.

   c) how individuals or organisations have worked for justice.

   Make sure you use the religious terms correctly here. You won't get the 6 marks if you muddle up Zakah and Sadaqah.

5) Say whether you agree with each of these statements.
   Give reasons for your answer, showing that you have thought of
   more than one point of view. You must refer to religious beliefs.

   a) "Truly religious people could never be racist."

   b) "Religion encourages discrimination against women."

   c) "Religious people are more likely to be socially responsible."

   Remember, you're not getting marks here for having the 'right' opinion — only for having the <u>reasons</u> to back it up. Don't forget, you need to look at the issue from <u>two points of view</u> if you're hoping to get the full 8 marks.

General

Believing in God

Millions of people across the world believe in some kind of <u>divine being</u> or '<u>god</u>'. They believe for various reasons — for some people, it's based on <u>personal religious experience</u>, but for others it's more <u>indirect</u>.

It Can Start with Your Upbringing or a Search for Meaning

1) If you were brought up by <u>religious parents</u> and your <u>upbringing</u> itself was based on <u>religious teaching</u>, it seems <u>more likely</u> that you would <u>believe</u> in a god. The same would apply if you grew up in a <u>religious community</u> where life was based on faith in one particular religion.

2) The presence of <u>religion in the world</u> may also have an influence. It could be that you are influenced by the <u>good work</u> that religion does in the world — whether it be for <u>individuals</u>, <u>communities</u> or those who are experiencing <u>suffering</u>.

Si never could figure out where his religious beliefs came from.

3) You may also be drawn to the <u>purpose</u> and <u>structure</u> it provides — or simply to the desire to have <u>something to believe in</u>.

4) The <u>search for meaning</u> is a major reason for people becoming interested in a particular religion. People want to find <u>answers</u> or find out why life is as it is, and they might believe religion can help.

Design: "Someone Must Have Designed the Universe"

1) Many people are convinced of the existence of a god by <u>design arguments</u>.

2) The idea here is that the <u>intricate workings</u> of the <u>Universe</u> (or of <u>life</u>) <u>can't</u> have come about by <u>random chance</u>. There must have been some kind of <u>designer</u> — and this designer was <u>God</u>.

3) But <u>not everyone</u> is convinced by these arguments...

4) <u>Non-religious ideas</u> about the origin of the world <u>might</u> lead a person to become an <u>agnostic</u> (someone who doesn't know whether or not there's a god — strictly, someone who believes it's <u>impossible to know</u> whether there's a god or not) or an <u>atheist</u> (someone who <u>rejects completely</u> the idea of a divine being).

Mr Darwin

5) These ideas include the theory of <u>evolution</u> (<u>Darwinism</u>) and the <u>Big Bang theory</u> (<u>cosmology</u>) (see p34).

Evil can Prevent People From Believing in God

1) No one can deny that there's a huge amount of <u>evil and suffering</u> in the world.

2) Some people can't believe that a God who is <u>good</u> would <u>allow</u> this to happen, and so come to the conclusion there <u>isn't</u> a God at all.

We Live in an Increasingly Secular Society

1) In a <u>secular society</u>, religion and government are kept <u>completely separate</u>.

2) People in a secular society are still <u>free</u> to follow whichever religious faith they choose, just as they're free to have nothing to do with religion. But the Government <u>won't</u> take religious views into account when setting laws, or fund schools that only take children of a particular faith, etc. Some people believe that this system is <u>fairer</u>, as it gives no advantage to followers of any particular religious faith.

3) But even in a largely secular society, religion can play an important role. Religions continue to provide community <u>traditions</u>, e.g., festivals like <u>Easter</u>, <u>Christmas</u> and <u>Hanukkah</u>.

4) Religion also provides believers with an <u>authority</u> on how they should behave. It can make people more likely to live <u>moral</u> lives and to obey the <u>law</u> — resulting in a more <u>peaceful</u> society.

5) It can bring people <u>together</u> and give them a sense of <u>community</u> — and even non-religious people can enjoy the <u>facilities</u>, <u>events</u> and <u>activities</u> offered by religious groups.

Looks like the jury's still out on this one...

<u>Religion</u>'s a <u>personal</u> thing — Bob believes cos <u>his mum</u> does, Sam <u>gazes at the stars</u> at night and reckons there <u>must be a god</u>, and Al <u>doesn't</u> believe <u>at all</u>. Make sure you <u>learn all these reasons</u> for believing (or not).

Religious Experiences

There are <u>loads of ways</u> people claim to <u>experience God</u>.
For believers, these religious experiences allow people to '<u>know</u>' God as he reveals himself to them.

Religious Experiences May Lead to Belief in a God

How God <u>reveals</u> his presence to the world is known as <u>revelation</u>. He does this in <u>different ways</u>...

1) <u>NUMINOUS</u>
This describes an <u>experience</u> that <u>inspires awe and wonder</u>, where someone can <u>feel God's presence</u>.
For example, a <u>beautiful view</u> or a <u>butterfly's wing</u> might convince you there must be a creator.

Nothing up my sleeves...

2) <u>MIRACLES</u>
Miracles are <u>amazing events</u> that <u>can't be explained</u> by the laws of <u>nature</u> or <u>science</u>. The Bible is full of accounts of <u>Jesus's miracles</u>.
People claim miracles still occur (miracles of <u>healing</u> at <u>Lourdes</u>, for example) and bring people to God.
Miracles are said to <u>show God's power</u> and presence.

3) <u>PRAYER</u>
Prayer is an attempt to <u>contact God</u> directly. It usually involves <u>words</u> and can be thought of as a <u>conversation</u> with God. A person might feel the presence of God in an <u>answered prayer</u> e.g. if an ill person they pray for is cured, or they are filled with a sense of <u>inner peace</u> or <u>wonder</u>.

4) <u>RELIGIOUS SCRIPTURE</u>
People can read <u>religious scripture</u> (e.g. the Bible, the Qur'an or the Torah), and feel that the nature of <u>God</u> has been <u>revealed</u>.

5) <u>CHARISMATIC PHENOMENA</u> (or Charismatic Worship)
Following <u>conversion</u>, a <u>Christian believer</u> may claim to have been "<u>touched by the Holy Spirit</u>" and begin '<u>speaking in tongues</u>' (unknown languages), having <u>visions</u> or <u>prophesying</u> (speaking a message from God). They may also sing, dance, shake or cry during worship.

<u>Conversion</u> refers to the <u>first time</u> a person <u>becomes a follower</u> of a god (although it can also be used when someone <u>changes their faith</u>). They might say they've been '<u>saved</u>' or '<u>born again</u>'.

BUT THERE ARE PLENTY OF SCEPTICS AROUND...

A <u>key concern</u> for <u>non-believers</u> is whether these experiences are <u>real</u>.

Sceptics argue that they're <u>just illusions</u> brought on by <u>religious hysteria</u> or a <u>desire to believe</u> in something. Or that events that <u>seem</u> miraculous can actually be explained by <u>science</u>.

Revelation can be General (for Everyone) or Special (a Personal Visit)

<u>General revelation</u> refers to <u>experiences</u> which are <u>available to everyone</u>, including:
1) acts of nature, conscience and morality,
2) religious scripture,
3) the work of religious leaders.

<u>Special revelation</u> describes experiences of <u>God revealing himself directly</u> to an <u>individual</u> or to a <u>select group</u>, e.g.:
1) visions,
2) dreams,
3) prophecies.

"I've got a revelation here for a Mr Smith..."

Revelations, eh... Wow. I mean, just imagine. It's just <u>mind-blowing</u>...

The Nature of God

General

God is generally thought of as the 'Ultimate Being'. No one can be quite sure exactly what He's like though...

Christians, Muslims and Jews have Similar Beliefs about God

Since Christianity and Islam both developed from Judaism, the basic concept of God (or Allah) is something that all three faiths share. God is believed to be:

> OMNIPOTENT: all-powerful — nothing is impossible for God.
>
> OMNISCIENT: all-knowing — knowing everything that we do, think or feel.
>
> OMNI-BENEVOLENT: all-loving and all-compassionate — he wants only what's best for us.

God Can Be Considered a 'Person' or an Idea

1) The term 'personal god' refers to God as a 'person' — albeit an almighty and divine person. God would be someone that supports and cares for us as a friend would, with human emotions like us. If this were the case, prayer would become part of our individual relationship — a 'conversation' with God.

2) The problem with this is that God is meant to be omnipresent (everywhere at once) — which poses the question of how a personal god can be everywhere at once.

3) The term 'impersonal god' refers to God as a concept, a force or an idea of goodness and light. The 'prime number' theory is often used to represent this idea of God — something that can't be divided or reduced.

4) The obvious problem here is how you can have a relationship with a force or an idea.

Where is God? — Within or Outside the Universe?

1) An 'immanent' God is a God who is in the world with us — a God who has taken an active role in the progress of human history and continues to do so.

2) The problem here is that an immanent God may appear small and fallible.

3) On the other hand, a 'transcendent' God is outside the world and doesn't directly act in human history.

4) This view of God makes him remote and separate from our experience on Earth. However, Christians who see God as transcendent might argue that it is they who do the work of God and that he is working through them.

5) Unfortunately, this definition is a bit too abstract for a lot of people to understand.

6) Religious believers (and Christians in particular) often try not to deal with extremes of any of these ideas, preferring instead to draw on different aspects for different occasions. Many would argue that God needs to be a blend of all of the above.

God May Have Been the "First Cause"

1) The Universe as we know it works on the principle of 'cause and effect' — so an event happening now was caused by an earlier event, which in turn was caused by an even earlier event and so on back through time.

2) If you trace this chain of cause and effect back in time, you find two possibilities:

> a) The chain goes back forever — i.e. the Universe has always existed, it's eternal.
>
> b) You eventually reach a starting point — an uncaused cause or 'First Cause'.

3) Some people argue that this 'First Cause' must have been God.

It all went a bit 'Sophie's World' on us there for a minute...

This is seriously tricky stuff — and not just for Religious Studies. These questions have been worrying loads of people for ages. But, tricky or not, you have to understand all these ideas to do well in that GCSE.

Topic Three — Looking For Meaning

Christianity & Judaism

Christian and Jewish Teaching on God

Christian and Jewish beliefs about God are similar, but there are some differences.

The Bible and The Torah Teach About God

1) The Bible is the Christian Scriptures. It's authoritative in guiding the beliefs of Christians — it helps them understand what God is like. It's made up of the Old and New Testaments.

2) The Roman Catholic Church also takes its beliefs from the Magisterium (the teaching of the Pope, his cardinals and bishops). The Pope is considered infallible on matters of faith — he can't be wrong.

3) The 'Jewish Bible' is the Tenakh — it's basically the same as the Old Testament, but in a different order. It has three groups of books: the Torah (laws given to Moses directly by God), the Nevi'im (the prophets, whose words were inspired by God), and the Ketuvim (a mix of psalms, proverbs and philosophy).

Judaism and Christianity say Similar Things about God...

1) As Christianity grew directly from Judaism, their basic concepts of God are very similar.

2) The Judeo-Christian God is usually seen as male (referred to as He or Father), omnipotent, omniscient and omni-benevolent (see previous page).

3) Christians and Jews share the belief that God has given us free will.

However, many Jews and Christians believe that our lives are predestined — we control individual actions, but not the ultimate outcome of our lives.

...but There are Some Big Differences

4) The biggest difference is the Christian belief in the Trinity. Jews never believed Christ was the Son of God.

5) Another key difference between Jewish and Christian teaching is that Jews are forbidden to draw or make images of God, as this is considered idolatry.

"Hear O Israel: the Lord our God, the Lord is One"

Most Jews believe these things about God. They believe God is...

...ONE	Jews believe there's only one God. The heading above comes from Deuteronomy 6:4.
...A PERSON	i.e. he's not just a 'force', but neither is he an old man with a beard. Human beings were made 'in his image' (but this needn't mean he looks like us).
...THE CREATOR	i.e. he made the Universe and everything in it.
...THE SUSTAINER	i.e. he didn't just create the Universe and then sit back — his energy keeps it going.
...HOLY	'Holy' means 'set apart' or 'completely pure'. God is so holy that some Jews won't write or say the word 'God' — they write G-d and say Hashem ('the Name') or Adonai ('the Lord').
...OMNIPRESENT	i.e. present throughout the whole Universe.
...THE LAWGIVER	Jewish tradition says 'God wrote himself into the Torah'.
...THE TRUE JUDGE	Jews believe they shall all face him one day, for death is not 'the end'.
...THE REDEEMER	Jews believe God is merciful. He will save his people from sin and suffering.

The Trinity is Explained Nicely in the Nicene Creed
no pun intended

1) The Christian idea of the Trinity is perhaps best expressed in the Nicene Creed:

> "We believe in one God, the Father, the almighty, maker of heaven and earth... We believe in one Lord, Jesus Christ, the only son of God... Of one being with the Father... We believe in the Holy Spirit... The giver of life... Who proceeds from the Father and the Son..."

2) God the Father might be described as the transcendent part of God, the Son as the immanent and personal part, and the Holy Spirit as the immanent yet impersonal part (see page 21).

3) Christians might describe the Father as the creator and judge, the Son (Jesus) as the human incarnation of God (and Messiah, or saviour), and the Holy Spirit as the presence of God, inspiring and guiding them.

Jews and Christians — separated at (the) birth...

I know, it's a jam-packed page, but it's all important. Write down a list of similarities and a list of differences.

Muslim Teaching on God

Islam

Islam <u>shares</u> a lot of history and beliefs with Judaism and Christianity.
But Muslims believe Islam is the "<u>final word of god</u>".

The Muslim name for God is Allah

1) For Muslims, God is called <u>Allah</u> — and the word '<u>Islam</u>' can be translated as meaning '<u>submission</u>' or '<u>surrender</u>' to <u>Allah</u>.

2) According to Islamic teaching, <u>Allah</u> is the <u>creator</u> of everything.

3) He is referred to by <u>ninety-nine names</u> in the Qur'an — these names tell you what <u>Muslims believe</u> about Allah and his power. They include:
<u>Al-Khaliq</u> — The <u>Creator</u>, <u>Ar-Rahman</u> — The <u>Merciful</u>, <u>Al-Aziz</u> — The <u>Almighty</u>.
He is also called The <u>Provider</u>, The <u>Just</u>, The <u>Maintainer</u>, The <u>Hearer</u> and The <u>Real Truth</u>.

The Qur'an is The Word of Allah

1) Muslims get their understanding of Allah from the <u>Qur'an</u>. They believe it contains the <u>exact words</u> of Allah, just as he revealed them to the <u>Prophet Muhammad</u>.

2) There's no arguing with the Qur'an — there's only <u>one version</u> of it, and it's regarded as <u>completely correct</u>. If the Qur'an says that Muslims should believe something, or do something, then a Muslim must do it.

3) Allah gave the Qur'an to the Prophet Muhammad in <u>Arabic</u>, so Muslims always read the Qur'an in Arabic to make sure that nothing is lost in translation (yep, that means they have to <u>learn</u> Arabic).

Allah is One — A Fundamental Principle of Islam

> "He is Allah, [who is] One, Allah, the Eternal Refuge. He neither begets nor is born, nor is there to Him any equivalent." Qur'an 112:1-4

Judaism and Christianity are monotheistic religions too.

1) This passage describes the <u>basic principle</u> that <u>Allah is one</u>. Islam is a <u>monotheistic</u> religion (it says there's only one god) and this belief in the oneness or the <u>unity of Allah</u> (called <u>Tawhid</u>) is a <u>fundamental</u> principle of Islam.

2) The ninety-nine revealed names sum up much of the nature of Allah. He is <u>loving</u> and <u>compassionate</u>, he is the <u>creator</u> and <u>judge</u> of all humans, and knows <u>everything</u> they do.

3) Muslims believe that Allah <u>cannot</u> be thought of in human terms — he is the <u>Supreme Being</u> and has <u>no equal</u>.

4) To Muslims, Allah is <u>both immanent</u> and <u>transcendent</u> (see page 21).
He is <u>transcendent</u> in that he is the <u>power behind the Universe</u> and is <u>outside</u>, above or beyond both <u>his creation</u> and <u>time</u> itself. His <u>immanence</u> is demonstrated in this passage:

In this passage 'We' refers to Allah and 'him' or 'his' refers to humankind.

> "We have already created man and know what his soul whispers to him, and We are closer to him than [his] jugular vein." Qur'an 50:16

5) Human lives are <u>predestined</u> by Allah — but humans do have <u>free will</u>. See page 30 for more on predestination and free will.

6) Allah is good and kind. However, there is a belief in a <u>devil</u> (called <u>Iblis</u> or <u>Shaytan</u>) who was <u>cast out by Allah</u> and tries to <u>lead people away</u> from him.
Some Muslims would argue that Allah <u>allows Shaytan</u> to use this power to <u>test and tempt</u> us — we have the <u>free will to resist</u>.

Immanent AND transcendent? — I Qur'an't get my head round it...

There's some <u>mind-boggling stuff</u> in these last few pages about what (one or more) god(s) is/are. But at the end of the day, it seems Christians, Jews and Muslims <u>all agree</u> on the <u>fundamentals</u> — that God/Allah is <u>supreme</u>, <u>all-powerful</u> and <u>all-knowing</u>, that our <u>lives are predestined</u> by him/her/it and that we have <u>free will</u>.

Christianity

Worship and Vocation in Christianity

Sunday is 'The Lord's Day' for Christians — the day when they're most likely to worship in church.
Worship is the religious person's way of expressing their love of, respect for, and devotion to a god or gods.

Worship in Church can take Many Forms

1) Christians can worship on their own, at any time, in any place. However, most Christians believe that it's also important to come together to worship collectively — usually in church.

2) Most churches have their main service on a Sunday morning. The exact form of worship will vary between denominations — it may be structured or spontaneous, but virtually all denominations use hymns or songs, Bible readings, and a sermon.

3) In Roman Catholic, Orthodox, and most Anglican churches it will be structured and liturgical (i.e. it will follow a pattern laid down in writing — with set prayers, and readings).

4) Methodists and other nonconformists have structured but non-liturgical services, e.g. following the 'hymn sandwich' pattern, where the service consists of hymns alternating with readings, prayers and a sermon.

5) Roman Catholic and Orthodox Sunday services always include Holy Communion (called Mass in the Roman Catholic tradition), and Anglican churches usually do.

6) Pentecostals, House Churches and other independent Christian fellowships may have spontaneous, often charismatic, worship (involving expressions of emotion, such as clapping and dancing).

Holy Communion Remembers the Last Supper

1) At the Last Supper, Jesus said that the bread and wine on the table represented his body and blood. The disciples were to eat and drink in remembrance of him whenever they ate together.

2) Roman Catholics believe in transubstantiation (i.e. the bread and wine used at Mass become the flesh and blood of Christ), and every Mass is considered to be a re-enactment of Christ's sacrifice.

3) Any leftover consecrated bread and wine must be consumed by a priest, or placed in a ciborium (a lidded chalice) inside a 'safe' called a tabernacle.

4) Most other Christians simply regard Holy Communion as symbolic, and the Salvation Army and the Quakers do not have Communion at all.

On discovering that he had to eat the leftovers, Father Donald quickly made the switch to Communion pizza.

You can Respond to God Through a Vocation

1) A vocation is something God calls someone to do — it's their 'calling in life'. It can be a job, but isn't always. God will have created them with special gifts and talents for their mission.

2) You'll probably know if something's your vocation — you'll feel drawn to it, then when you're doing it, you'll feel 'at home'. But vocations are meant to be challenging rather than the easy option. Christians believe you need God's help to do them.

3) There are lots of different vocations a Christian might be called to. Here are a few examples:

- joining a religious order as a monk or a nun, to live a life of prayer and contemplation.
- a life of serving the Church, perhaps by training to be a priest.
- missionary work — trying to convert people to Christianity, maybe in a remote part of the world.
- a non-religious job such as a doctor, teacher or social worker, in order to help people.
- volunteering in the community — e.g. running a youth group.
- charity work — either religion-based (e.g. Christian Aid), or secular (e.g. Greenpeace).
- marriage and raising children.

4) Non-religious people often feel they have a 'vocation' too — they just don't believe that God called them to it.

5) You have to actually choose to follow your vocation — it doesn't just happen.

I'd like a hymn and mustard sandwich please...

Don't get vocations muddled up with vacations. God is probably not going to be calling you to go and lounge on a beach in Benidorm for two weeks. Learn all this stuff about how people respond to God.

Worship and Vocation in Judaism

The Jewish holy day is the <u>Shabbat</u> (<u>Sabbath</u>), but in Judaism, prayer is important every day of the week.

There are Three Special Times for Daily Prayer

1) <u>Prescribed</u> daily prayers happen at three special times — in the <u>morning</u>, <u>afternoon</u> and <u>evening</u>.

2) At these times, <u>men</u> will try to attend the <u>synagogue</u> and become part of a <u>minyan</u> — a group of at least ten men, which is the minimum needed for a service. <u>Women</u> (traditionally because of their domestic commitments) are trusted to pray <u>at home</u>.

3) As well as the normal daily prayers, there are also special prayers for when getting up and going to bed, before and after eating... in fact, pretty much <u>every</u> event in life, good or bad, can be a reason to pray.

Shabbat (Sabbath) is Celebrated in the Synagogue...

The Sabbath is a day of rest to commemorate the <u>7th Day of Creation</u> when God rested after making the Universe. It begins at <u>sunset</u> on Friday, and ends on Saturday evening when <u>stars</u> begin to appear.

There are three separate <u>services</u> in the synagogue on the Sabbath.

`FRIDAY EVENING` Shabbat is welcomed with singing led by a <u>chazan</u> (cantor).
No instruments are used — this is a <u>symbol</u> of mourning for the destruction of the Temple in Jerusalem.

The chazan's role is to lead the singing and chant prayers.

`SATURDAY MORNING` — the <u>main</u> service of the week. The <u>rabbi</u> will read from the Torah and give a sermon. Also, seven men are called up to read or recite a blessing, and an eighth reads a portion from the Nevi'im. In Orthodox synagogues, women sit <u>separately</u> from the men and take little part.

See p.22

`SATURDAY AFTERNOON` this service includes a reading from the <u>Torah</u>, and three special <u>prayers</u>.

...and in the Home

1) A special <u>Shabbat meal</u> is eaten — accompanied by lots of <u>rituals</u>, such as lighting candles, reciting from the Torah, and saying blessings.

2) Much of the <u>food</u> eaten at the Shabbat meal is <u>symbolic</u>.

<u>Wine</u> is used to symbolise the sweetness and joy of Shabbat.

<u>Challot</u> are eaten — these are two plaited loaves which commemorate the double portion of '<u>manna</u>' which God provided the day before each Shabbat during the <u>Exodus</u>.

The Exodus is when Moses led the Israelite slaves from Egypt to freedom.

The Covenant Gave Jewish People Their Chief Vocation

1) The <u>covenant</u> is the <u>contract</u> that God has made with the Jewish people. It commits them to <u>serving God</u> and to living as the <u>Torah</u> says they should. Many Jewish people consider this their <u>vocation</u> in life.

2) The Hebrew phrase '<u>Tikkun Olam</u>' means '<u>mending the world</u>' (see page 36). Jews are all expected to join in this task, although they can't complete it alone.

3) Jewish people may also share many of the same vocations as Christians, e.g. <u>marriage</u> and having <u>children</u> is considered very important in Judaism.

"Be fruitful and increase in number; fill the earth..." Genesis 1:28

4) Jewish people can train for religious jobs — for example, as a <u>rabbi</u> or as a <u>chazan</u>. (Although in Orthodox Judaism, only men are allowed in these roles.)

Louise hoped that the 'lemon look' would catch on.

5) Jewish people don't believe that they need to convert people to Judaism — so missionary work <u>wouldn't</u> be a Jewish vocation.

This page must seem like manna from heaven...

Ho, ho, ho... anyway, the bit about worship describes the behaviour of observant Orthodox Jews. Progressive Jews tend to have a more relaxed attitude to exactly when Shabbat should begin and end, etc.

Islam

Worship and Vocation in Islam

To a Muslim <u>all life</u> is worship. Every part of life is lived in a way that will please Allah and show obedience to him. If it's done with Allah in mind, then it's <u>worship</u>. It all comes down to the <u>Five Pillars</u> of Islam.

Muslim Worship is all about the Five Pillars

1

SHAHADAH — the Muslim Declaration of Faith

"There is no god but Allah, and Muhammad is the Prophet of Allah."
Muslims should repeat this <u>several times a day</u> — and they should pray only to Allah.

2

SALAH — Prayer five times a day

1) You can't be a Muslim without <u>praying</u> in the way Muhammad did. Regular prayer keeps Allah in a Muslim's mind. It also keeps Muslims aware of their <u>duty</u> to obey Allah.

2) The <u>muezzin</u> makes the call to prayer (<u>adhan</u>) from the <u>minaret</u> of a <u>mosque</u>. ➤

3) <u>Wudu</u> (washing before prayer) is important. This is because a Muslim must be <u>pure</u> and <u>clean</u> when approaching Allah.

4) A Muslim should face <u>Makkah</u> (Muhammad's place of birth) when praying.

5) There is a set <u>ritual</u> for prayer — each unit of prayer is known as a <u>rak'ah</u> (and the rak'ah may be repeated <u>several</u> times at each prayer session). Each rak'ah involves <u>standing</u>, then <u>kneeling</u>, then putting your <u>forehead</u> to the ground to symbolise submission.

6) If several Muslims are praying in one place, then they all do the ritual <u>together</u> to symbolise <u>unity</u>.

7) <u>Friday</u> prayers are called <u>Salah-al-Jum'ah</u> (or just <u>Jum'ah</u>) — it's a community occasion, and at least 40 people should be there, all praying together.

Salah is <u>compulsory</u> prayer. Extra prayers are called <u>Du'a</u>, and Muslims can do these at <u>any time</u>. In Du'a prayers, <u>beads</u> can be used — 99 beads to symbolise the 99 names of Allah.

3

ZAKAH — Giving money or possessions to help the poor, sick and needy — See page 12.

4

SAWM — Obligation to fast in Ramadan

<u>Ramadan</u> is the 9th month of the Muslim calendar, and celebrates Muhammad first receiving the revelation of the <u>Qur'an</u>. No food or drink can pass your lips during daylight hours. This <u>fasting</u> teaches self-discipline, which is believed to draw Muslims closer to Allah.

5

HAJJ — Pilgrimage to Makkah at least once in your life (if you're healthy and wealthy enough)

This journey-of-a-lifetime demonstrates a Muslim's <u>devotion</u> to Allah. Those on a pilgrimage all wear <u>simple</u>, <u>plain garments</u>, showing that everyone's <u>equal</u> before Allah — wealth and status <u>don't matter</u>.

The Greater Jihad is the Vocation of a Muslim

1) <u>The Greater</u>, or <u>Internal</u>, <u>Jihad</u> is the personal <u>struggle</u> of a Muslim to live their faith as best they can — it involves fighting their own desires in order to please Allah.

2) This means following all the rules making up the <u>Five Pillars</u>, being totally devoted to Allah, living as he commanded, and doing everything they can to <u>help other people</u>.

3) For a Muslim, the Greater Jihad may involve anything from learning the Qur'an by heart, to <u>volunteering</u> in the community, or perhaps becoming an <u>imam</u> (an imam is often a community leader as well as a spiritual leader).

4) Pleasing Allah is really important to a Muslim — if someone pleases Allah enough, they'll be sent to <u>Paradise</u> on Judgement Day.

The Qur'an doesn't cover every detail of how Muslims should live. Extra day-to-day guidance is found in the law-code called the <u>shari'ah</u>. This is based on Islamic tradition, as well as religious texts, and covers modern issues, such as drugs.

Makkah, Zakah and Rak'ah — this page is a cracker... *boom boom...*

As with many things in Muslim life, the Five Pillars have their basis in the <u>Qur'an</u> and the <u>life of Muhammad</u>. For example, the zakah is supposed to reflect Muhammad's <u>generosity</u> during his lifetime.

Symbolism in Religion

Imagery and symbolism are visible signs of invisible ideas — which all religions are packed with.

Christianity is Packed With Symbolism

The most common Christian symbol is the cross — it's a reminder of the crucifixion and resurrection of Jesus. There are plenty more too...

1 Icons are paintings (mostly of saints) found in Orthodox churches. They're often greeted with a kiss on entering the building. They're used to represent the presence of saints, and as a means to pray.

3 The dove is a symbol used to represent the holy spirit, and the idea of peace. A dove appeared at Jesus's baptism.

2 Orthodox churches are often in the shape of a cross, with a large dome on top symbolising Christ's presence, eternity and the nearness of heaven.

4 Christians often put a fish symbol on the back of their cars to show their faith. The fish symbol was a secret sign used when Christians were being persecuted. It was chosen because the initial letters of the Greek for 'Jesus Christ, God's son, saviour' spell out the Greek word for 'fish'.

And Judaism Has Loads Too

Symbols of the Jewish faith are the menorah (a seven-branched candlestick) or a magen David (a six pointed star). There are plenty of others though...

Some food is symbolic in Judaism — see page 25.

1 The mezuzah is a sign which is put on doors in Jewish houses to remind the family of the covenant (the two-way promise that God made with Abraham and Moses). It's a tiny parchment scroll containing words from the Torah in Hebrew. It's put inside a case to keep it safe. It comes from an instruction in Deuteronomy 6:6-9.

2 Many Jewish men and boys wear a small cap called a kippah as a sign of respect to God. It reminds them that God's intelligence is vastly higher than ours.

3 The Tefillin (or Phylacteries) are worn during morning prayers, except on the Sabbath and on festival days. They're two leather boxes, one worn on the upper arm (next to the heart), one on the head. Inside are tiny scrolls containing Torah passages. These remind Jews to serve God with head and heart — the command to wear them also comes from Deuteronomy 6:6-9.

A Mosque (or Masjid) is the Muslim House of Prayer

Islam doesn't have too many symbols — but there's some other imagery worth mentioning...

1) Some mosques are extremely simple, others are very grand, but all have a dome symbolising the Universe.

2) A special niche (called the mihrab) in the 'direction-wall' shows the direction in which Makkah lies (the direction which Muslims pray towards).

"Muhammad" **"Allah"**

3) There are no pictures of Muhammad or Allah, since no one is allowed to draw them. But Arabic characters are used by represent them.

4) The colour green is traditionally used in mosques. This is believed to be because it was Muhammad's favourite colour (he's thought to have had a green turban and banner), and because it symbolises life.

There's something fishy here — must be my kippah...

You definitely need to know about symbols in religion. There's just no getting away from that. It's like trying to get away with passing your maths exam without really getting to grips with what a 'number' is.

General & Christianity

Life After Death: Christianity

What people believe will happen to them after <u>death</u> can influence the way they <u>live</u> their lives.

Life After Death — Some People Believe, Others Don't

1) Some people believe that when you die, that's it — your body decays and you <u>cease to exist</u>.

2) Others believe that, although your <u>body</u> may die and decay, your <u>soul</u> (the spiritual part of you) can live on — in other words, you move on to a different kind of existence (an <u>afterlife</u>). This is the basic idea of <u>life after death</u>.

Life After Death is Very Important to Lots of People

1) Most <u>religions</u> teach that we all move on to an <u>afterlife</u> of some kind. For some people, this will be enough to make them believe in life after death — they have <u>faith</u> in what their religion teaches.

2) Pretty much everyone knows they're going to die one day — and for many it's a hard concept to grasp, and death is a <u>scary</u> thought. Many people get a lot of <u>comfort</u> from a belief in the afterlife.

3) Also, when someone you love dies, it's a lot nicer to think that they <u>still exist</u> in some form.

4) Belief in life after death is also important from a <u>justice</u> point of view. Lots of good people <u>suffer</u> greatly, and some, sadly, die young. At the same time, some <u>evil</u> people live out long lives quite happily. It can make people feel a lot better if they believe that everything will be <u>evened up</u> after death.

5) Christianity, Judaism and Islam all have an afterlife reward/punishment system with <u>eternal life in paradise</u> for the goodies, and <u>punishment</u> for the baddies (or perhaps just missing out on eternal life).

The religions all differ in what you have to do to qualify as a goody though.

6) So belief in an afterlife might be a <u>reason</u> for some people to <u>follow a religion</u> or do <u>good deeds</u> — they want to make sure they're well qualified for a good afterlife.

7) <u>Non-religious people</u> may believe in some sort of afterlife too — they might still think there's more to life than just the physical.

Christian Teaching — Heaven and Hell

1) Christianity teaches that the <u>soul</u> lives on after death (<u>immortality</u> of the soul), and that the body will be <u>resurrected</u> (brought back to life) for Judgement Day, just as Jesus was resurrected after his crucifixion.

2) Christians believe that you'll go either to <u>Heaven</u>, or to <u>Hell</u>:

- Heaven is often portrayed as a place of great beauty and serenity, a <u>paradise</u> where you'll spend eternity with God — as long as you believe in <u>Jesus</u>, have followed his teachings and have lived a <u>good</u> life, that is. Those in Heaven are said to belong to the <u>Communion of Saints</u>.

- Hell, on the other hand, is often portrayed as a place of <u>torment</u> and <u>pain</u> — the final destination of <u>nonbelievers</u> and those who have led <u>bad</u> lives.

And in Hell they make you wear bad wigs and false moustaches... <u>forever</u>.

3) However, not all Christians believe that these are <u>real</u> places — many Christians see Heaven and Hell as <u>states of mind</u>. In Heaven you'll be <u>happy</u>, and know God — in Hell you'll be <u>unable</u> to know God's love.

4) A few believe those who God finds unacceptable will be <u>annihilated</u>. They had no interest in spiritual things when they were <u>alive</u>, therefore their spirits were never awakened and cannot survive death.

5) Roman Catholics also believe in a place, or state of existence, called <u>Purgatory</u>. Here <u>sins</u> are punished before the soul is able to move on to Heaven. This concept isn't in the Bible though, so Protestants reject it.

6) The fear of punishment or promise of rewards in the afterlife <u>encourages</u> believers to live <u>good lives</u>. But many Christians believe even those who led sinful lives may find <u>salvation</u> thanks to God's saving power.

Get ready to do some soul searching...

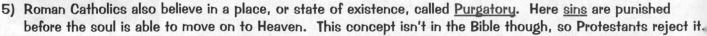

I wonder if we're all destined to an afterlife of moving people's car keys and eating socks? Mmm... socks...

Life After Death: Judaism

Judaism

It should come as no surprise at all to learn that Judaism has something to say about <u>life after death</u> as well.

Sheol — the Shadowy Destination of the Dead

1) Jewish teachings are largely concerned with the <u>earthly</u> life, and a person's <u>duties</u> to God and other people. According to the Torah, rewards for obeying God and punishments for 'breaking the covenant' are sent in <u>this world</u>.

2) But Jews still have a firm belief in the <u>immortality of the soul</u>.

3) When the earliest Jewish scriptures were written, it was believed that after death <u>all souls</u> went to a place called <u>Sheol</u> — where the dead lived as shadows. Sheol was believed to be dark and cold, and your soul would stay there for <u>eternity</u>. This <u>wasn't</u> as a punishment — it's just what was believed to happen.

4) However, over time the Jews came to believe in the <u>resurrection</u> of the dead...

> *"If you follow my decrees... I will send you rain in its season, and the ground will yield its crops and the trees of the field their fruit... and you will eat all the food you want and live in safety in your land. I will grant peace in the land, and you will lie down and no one will make you afraid... and I will keep my covenant with you.*
>
> *But if you will not listen to me... and abhor my laws ... and so violate my covenant... I will bring upon you sudden terror, wasting diseases and fever that will destroy your sight and drain away your life. You will plant seed in vain... I will set my face against you... those who hate you will rule over you..."* Leviticus 26:3-17.

In the Messianic Age the Dead Will be Resurrected

1) Jews believe that the <u>Messiah</u>, a great future leader, will bring an era of <u>perfect peace</u> and <u>prosperity</u> called the <u>World to Come</u> (or <u>messianic age</u>). (Jews don't believe Jesus was the Messiah.)

> *"Multitudes who sleep in the dust of the earth will awake: some to <u>everlasting life</u>, others to shame and <u>everlasting contempt</u>."* Daniel 12:2.

2) It's believed that the <u>righteous</u> dead (both Jews and non-Jews) will be <u>resurrected</u> to share in the messianic peace. But the <u>wicked</u> dead won't be resurrected.

3) Orthodox Jews believe that the <u>physical body</u> will be resurrected, <u>intact</u>, in the messianic age. Because of this, the body shouldn't be cut after death (<u>autopsies</u> are frowned upon) and cremation is <u>forbidden</u>. A Jewish cemetery is called the '<u>House of Life</u>' (Bet ha-Chaim), which reaffirms the view that the body will be resurrected.

4) Reform Jews believe that the body is simply a <u>vessel</u> for the soul, and <u>reject</u> the idea of physical resurrection. So Reform Jews accept cremation and organ donation.

Okay, it was wrong. But everlasting contempt seems a bit over the top.

Modern Judaism Teaches of Gan Eden and Gehinnom

1) Modern Jews believe in an afterlife spent in places called <u>Gan Eden</u> ("Garden of Eden" or Paradise) and <u>Gehinnom</u> (a bit like Purgatory), but they don't tend to have firm beliefs on the <u>specifics</u> of the afterlife.

2) Some see Gan Eden as a <u>physical</u> place of lavish banquets and warm sunshine. But others have a more <u>spiritual</u> view of it — as a <u>closeness</u> to God. Similarly, there are different views of Gehinnom — a place of fire and physical <u>torment</u>, or a chance to see your <u>missed opportunities</u> and the <u>harm</u> you caused in life.

3) Only if you've lived a <u>blameless</u> life will you be sent straight to Gan Eden when you die.

4) Most souls are sent to Gehinnom for a period of <u>punishment</u> and <u>purification</u> first, which many think lasts no longer than <u>12 months</u>, before ascending to Gan Eden. Only the <u>truly wicked</u> never reach Paradise, but there are various ideas about what happens to them, e.g. they're annihilated, or they stay in Gehinnom forever.

The Shadows — they used to be Cliff Richard's band...

Yep, in the old days, when <u>Cliff Richard</u> was a young rock 'n' roll singer (well before he started doing all that <u>Christmas nonsense</u>), he had a backing band called the <u>Shadows</u>. But an eternity spent listening to Cliff Richard songs probably isn't what early Jews had in mind when they came up with Sheol...

Islam

Life After Death: Islam

Islam, like other religions, has very definite teachings when it comes to life after death.

Akhirah — Life After Death

1) Muslims call life after death <u>akhirah</u> — it's one of the key Islamic beliefs.
Not to have a belief in life after death would make <u>this</u> life meaningless for a Muslim.

Only Allah knows why he tests us in these ways.

2) Islam teaches that nothing that happens to us during our earthly lives is <u>accidental</u> — Muslims believe we are being <u>tested</u>, and that the way we act in life will determine what happens to us after we die.

3) A key teaching of Islam is that we remain in the grave after death in a state called <u>barzakh</u> (the <u>cold sleep</u>) until the <u>Day of Judgement</u>. On this day, Allah will judge <u>everyone</u> — not just Muslims.

The Soul Goes to al'Jannah (Paradise) or Jahannam (Hell)

1) Although the <u>earthly</u> life is short compared with the eternal, Muslims believe it's still very important.
It's in this life that Allah <u>tests</u> us. On <u>Judgement Day</u>, it's <u>too late</u> to beg forgiveness for any wrongdoing.

2) Islam teaches we are judged on:
  i) our <u>character</u>,
  ii) our <u>reactions</u> to good and bad events in life,
  iii) our <u>way of life</u>.

3) Muslims believe everything is the <u>will of Allah</u> — so there's no point <u>moaning</u> about your circumstances.
We cannot know <u>why</u> things happen, or what Allah wishes us to learn from it.
The important thing is that we react to it the <u>right</u> way.

4) The reward for those who have followed Allah will be entry into <u>al'Jannah</u> (<u>Paradise</u>) — this is a place of peace, happiness and beauty. In fact, the Qur'an refers to al'Jannah as '<u>gardens of delight</u>', filled with flowers and birdsong.

5) For those who don't <u>believe</u> in Allah, or have committed bad deeds, the reward is <u>Jahannam</u> (or <u>Hell</u>). The Qur'an describes Jahannam as a place of scorching <u>fire</u>, hot <u>winds</u> and black <u>smoke</u>. Here, those who have ignored Allah's teaching and failed to act righteously will be <u>punished</u> for eternity.

6) But Allah is also <u>merciful</u>, so many of those who have lived <u>sinful</u> lives may not be sent to Jahannam.

> Allah is merciful and compassionate, but at the same time, he's a tough judge. Basically, if you're a good Muslim, you'll go to Paradise. If you're a bad Muslim or a non-Muslim, you deserve Hell, but you might get lucky and be sent by Allah to Paradise if he's feeling merciful.

The Soul is the Real Person

1) Muslims believe human beings are Allah's <u>greatest</u> physical creation. They also believe that humans are different from other animals, because we know we will <u>die</u>.

2) Islam teaches that every <u>soul</u> (<u>ruh</u>) is unique and has <u>free will</u>.

3) On Judgement Day, it is the soul that will be <u>resurrected</u> and <u>judged</u>, as it is the soul that is our <u>consciousness</u>. Our body is thought of as a kind of 'vehicle for the soul'.

> It's <u>free will</u> that makes human beings different from <u>angels</u> — angels obey Allah <u>perfectly</u>.

> Muslims believe in predestination — Al-Qadr. Although we have free will, Islam teaches we cannot do everything we want — God is still in control. In recognition of this, Muslims will often say "insh' Allah" (if God is willing).

Stop moaning about your Exam — it is the will of Allah...

Don't be put off by the long and difficult words on this page — just get learning and your RS exam will fly by. Don't worry, there's only another three pages to go in this section... (...what did I say about the moaning...)

Funeral Rites: Christianity

Funeral rites are important in most religions. They're for both the dead person <u>and</u> for the bereaved.

Funeral Customs help Support the Bereaved

1) A funeral gives people an <u>opportunity</u> to express their <u>love and respect</u> for the deceased. It helps them with the <u>grieving process</u>.

2) Funeral services usually have a great deal to say about the hope of <u>eternal life</u>. The bereaved people are encouraged to believe that one day they'll be <u>reunited</u> with the deceased.

3) Funerals are often considered <u>celebrations</u> of the life of the deceased — they focus on all the special things about the person.

Funeral Services are Sad, but with a note of Hope

Funeral services <u>vary</u> according to denomination, but all Christian funerals contain a note of <u>hope</u>. For many this doesn't mean wishful thinking — it means confident <u>expectation</u> based on God's promises.

1) The <u>coffin</u> is carried into the church, and words from <u>John 11</u> are often read. There are <u>hymns</u>, other <u>Bible readings</u> and <u>prayers</u>. The priest (or someone else) often gives a short <u>sermon</u> about Christian belief in life after death, and may also talk about the <u>life</u> of the person who has died.

> "I am the resurrection and the life. He who believes in me will live, even though he dies; and whoever lives and believes in me will never die." John 11:25-26

2) Of course there will be <u>sadness</u> too, particularly if the person died young or very suddenly. There are <u>prayers</u> for the bereaved, and members of the congregation will express their sympathy for the family and close friends of the deceased. <u>Black</u> clothes are often worn, though some Christians consider this <u>inappropriate</u> and may even request that guests don't dress in this way.

3) Here are some of the special features of <u>Roman Catholic</u> and <u>Orthodox</u> funerals:

Orthodox Funeral

1) After the person dies, their body is <u>washed and dressed</u> and placed in an <u>open coffin</u> at the altar.
2) A piece of material showing <u>icons</u> of Jesus, Mary and John the Baptist is placed over the forehead.
3) A <u>linen cloth</u> is placed over the coffin to <u>symbolise</u> Jesus's protection.

Roman Catholic Funeral

1) The coffin is often brought into the church <u>the night before</u> and prayers are said.
2) The funeral includes Holy Communion (the '<u>Requiem Mass</u>'). The purpose of a Requiem Mass is to pray for the soul of the dead person, particularly while it's in <u>Purgatory</u>. The priest wears <u>white</u> vestments, and the coffin is covered with a white cloth (a <u>pall</u>) — white is symbolic of life after death.
3) The coffin is sprinkled with <u>holy water</u> and the priest says, "*In the waters of baptism (name) died with Christ, and rose with him to new life. May s/he now share with him in eternal glory.*" The coffin is later sprinkled again, and also perfumed with <u>incense</u>.

The Body Might Be Buried or Cremated

Orthodox Christians are opposed to cremation.

1) It doesn't matter to most Christians whether the body's <u>buried</u> or <u>cremated</u> — Christians believe that at the Resurrection they'll have new 'spiritual bodies'.
   - A memorial stone, which families may visit in the future, will usually be erected to mark a grave.
   - Ashes from cremations are often scattered in a special, beautiful place.

2) There'll be another service at the <u>graveside</u> or <u>crematorium</u>. The final words are often:

> "Earth to earth, ashes to ashes, dust to dust; in sure and certain hope of the resurrection to eternal life through our Lord Jesus Christ, who died, was buried and rose again for us."

3) Afterwards, there'll usually be a <u>meal</u> for family and friends.

Hmm... Perhaps a bit premature...

Hmmm — there's no fun in funerals...

Phew — bit depressing is this stuff. But Christians try not to see death as <u>depressing</u> — after all, they believe the person who died is <u>going to Heaven</u> (probably), which has to be a good thing, if you're a Christian. Of course, it'd be a bit of a downer if you thought they might go to Hell, but let's not dwell on that.

Funeral Rites: Judaism and Islam

Judaism & Islam

Jewish life is filled with rituals, so it's not surprising they have plenty for when someone dies.

Judaism has Customs to Comfort the Bereaved...

① Jewish families <u>gather</u> near a loved one who is dying, while the dying person spends their last moments confessing <u>sins</u> and reciting the <u>Shema</u> (one of the most important Jewish prayers).

② After the death, each family member makes a small <u>tear</u> in their clothing — a symbol of grief and shock.

③ The dead person must not be left alone until they're <u>buried</u> (<u>not</u> cremated — see page 29). This must be done as soon as possible, preferably within <u>24 hours</u>.

④ The body's washed and might then be ritually cleansed in a <u>mikveh</u> (a Jewish ritual bath). Then it's wrapped in a white linen <u>shroud</u>, before being placed in a plain, unpolished, wooden <u>coffin</u> to show that in death, rich and poor are <u>equal</u>. This is done by a Chevra Kaddisha (burial society).

⑤ At the funeral service in the synagogue, <u>psalms</u> are read and a prayer is said praising God for giving life and for taking it away. The rabbi might make a short speech about the deceased.

⑥ Everyone throws a <u>spadeful of earth</u> into the grave — this symbolises that the body is being returned to the earth.

Flowers aren't left on Jewish graves — stones are left instead.

⑦ The first week after the funeral is called <u>shiva</u> (seven). The immediate family stay at home and are <u>visited</u> by relatives and friends who pray with them three times a day and offer comfort. They do not cut their hair, shave, listen to music or have sex. The men recite a prayer called the <u>kaddish</u>. Everyone is encouraged to talk about the person who has died.

⑧ The first month after the funeral is called <u>Sheloshim</u> (thirty). During this time, life returns <u>gradually</u> to normal, and male mourners go to the synagogue to recite the <u>kaddish</u>. Anyone who has lost a parent remains <u>in mourning</u> for a whole <u>year</u>.

⑨ The anniversary of death is called <u>Yahrzeit</u>. It is on the first yahrzeit that a <u>headstone</u> will usually be erected above the grave. Every year a candle is lit for 24 hours and men say the <u>kaddish</u>.

...And So does Islam

① A Muslim hopes <u>not</u> to die <u>alone</u>, but with relatives and friends around, who'll keep them <u>company</u> and look after them. They might also read the Qur'an and pray. They'll also <u>recite</u> 'There is no God but Allah' — these should be the <u>last words</u> a Muslim says or hears.

② After a person has died, the body is <u>washed</u> three times by family members and <u>perfume</u> is applied. The body is then <u>wrapped</u> in a clean white <u>shroud</u>.

③ The funeral takes place within 24 hours. Although everyone attends the prayers in the mosque, only men go with the body to the graveside. <u>Funeral prayers</u> (Janazah prayers) are said, praying that the dead person may be judged <u>mercifully</u> and gain a place in <u>Paradise</u>. The body is <u>buried</u> in a simple grave, lying on its <u>right side</u> facing <u>Makkah</u>.

It's said that graves are visited by two <u>angels</u> to question the deceased and work out whether they're fit for the <u>next life</u>.

④ Lavish memorials aren't set up — simple grave markers are used instead. A period of <u>mourning</u> is kept for <u>three days</u>, finishing with Qur'an reading and prayers. Widows are expected to mourn for 4 months and 10 days.

You need a big hole to bury a goldfish — if it's inside a cat...

Don't forget, Jewish and Muslim folk don't believe that death is the end — like Christians, they believe in an <u>afterlife</u> (see pages 28-30). Anyway, make sure you learn all the <u>funeral rites</u> on this page. The best way is to shut the book and scribble them out <u>from memory</u> — then check back to see which ones you missed.

Practice Questions

You're right... there's some heavy stuff in this section. And a lot of it is about things that no one can know for sure, like the nature of God/Allah, and what happens after death. But the religions all have strong beliefs on these matters and you need to know what they are. And then there are the funeral rites to learn... It's not cheery, but there are only two things that are certain in life — death and exams.

So try your hand at these questions. And keep trying them until you can do them all without breaking into even the mildest of sweats.

1) Explain what religious believers mean by:
   a) God.
   b) revelation.
   c) numinous.
   d) charismatic phenomena.
   e) miracle.
   f) omnipotent.
   g) immanent.
   h) afterlife.
   i) vocation.
   j) First Cause.
   k) free will.
   l) Tawhid. *(Islam)*

These "definition" questions are worth 2 marks each in the exam, so make sure you give a full definition. Try the glossary at the back of the book if you're struggling.

2) Explain how:
   a) a religious person might feel that God has revealed Himself to them.
   b) a religious person might respond to God through their vocation.
   c) belief in an afterlife might affect how someone lives.
   d) funeral rites might help or comfort a bereaved person.

You don't need to give a balanced argument for these questions. Just show that you know the religious facts and explanations.

3) Give two reasons why a religious believer might agree or disagree with each of these statements:
   a) "The Universe was designed by God."
   b) "Religion has no value in a secular society."
   c) "God fully controls our lives."

These questions aren't asking for a big list of different reasons, just two. Each reason's worth 2 marks in the exam — so make sure you expand on each one.

4) Explain, from two different religious traditions:
   a) the use of symbolism.
   b) the mourning and funeral rites.
   c) teachings about the afterlife.

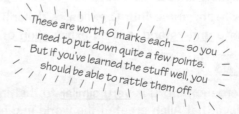

These are worth 6 marks each — so you need to put down quite a few points. But if you've learned the stuff well, you should be able to rattle them off.

5) Say whether you agree with each of these statements. Give reasons for your answer, showing that you have thought of more than one point of view. You must refer to religious beliefs.
   a) "It is impossible to know whether God exists."
   b) "Worship is the most important part of religion."
   c) "It doesn't matter if life is unfair, it gets evened up in the end."

This lot of questions should remind you that you need to learn both sides of the big arguments — no matter how passionately you believe in your own opinion. There are 8 marks up for grabs here.

Christianity, Judaism, Islam & General

Origins of the World and Life

No one saw exactly how the Earth came to be like it is... but science and religion both have their theories.

Scientific Arguments — There are Two Main Types

COSMOLOGICAL THEORIES — How the Universe came into being

Chief amongst these is the Big Bang theory. It says that the Universe began in an explosion of matter and energy. Matter from this explosion eventually formed stars, planets and everything else. The Universe still seems to be expanding today — important evidence for this theory.

EVOLUTIONARY THEORIES — How living things came to be like they are today

In 1859, Charles Darwin published 'On the Origin of the Species'. In this book he argued that all life on the planet originated from simple cells. Life evolved (gradually changed) over millions of years into a huge variety of forms. According to this theory, we evolved from apes — not from Adam and Eve.

These theories are at odds with many religious arguments. However, if you don't take everything in the Bible or Torah literally, scientific and religious ideas can exist in harmony. Science tells us how, religion tells us why.

Religions have their Own Ideas about all this...

Christian Ideas

"In the beginning God created the heavens and the earth." Genesis 1:1

1) Traditional Christian and Jewish teachings about Creation come from the same scriptures, and so are identical.

2) According to Genesis Chapter 1, God created everything. If the Bible is taken literally, the process took six days, and humankind didn't evolve from apes, but is descended from Adam and Eve.

3) However, some Christians view Genesis as a parable, or as a symbolic description of a more gradual evolution. So it's possible to believe in the Bible and science.

4) In 1996 the Roman Catholic Church accepted the Big Bang theory — definitely a significant acceptance of science.

The Creation in Genesis Chapter 1

Genesis says things were created in the following order: on the first day light and darkness; on the second day the sky; on the third day oceans, land and plants on the land; on the fourth day the sun, moon and stars; on the fifth day creatures of the water and sky (e.g. fish and birds); and then on the sixth day, land animals and people. On the seventh day, God rested.

If you ignore the fourth day, this is pretty much the same order as scientists think things appeared. So the timescale is different (millions of years rather than six days), but the general idea is the same.

Jewish Ideas

1) Orthodox Jews, who see the Torah as the word of God and so literally true, would find it difficult to accept scientific arguments about creation.

2) Reform Jews might argue that Creation as described in the Torah is more a way for us to understand, not an explanation of, how it happened.

Yeah, not bad. I reckon I deserve a day off.

Islamic Ideas

1) The Muslim creation story is very similar to that in Genesis. Muslims believe that Allah created the world and everything in it.

2) But descriptions of creation in the Qur'an aren't entirely at odds with science. In fact, scientific theories are supported by passages like this.

3) Islam differs from science when it comes to the creation of humans, though. The Qur'an states that Allah formed Adam from clay and breathed life and a soul into him. And that all humans descend from Adam.

"Have those who disbelieved not considered that the heavens and the earth were a joined entity, and We separated them and made from water every living thing? Then will they not believe?" Qur'an 21:30

In the beginning, God created exams...

Albert Einstein once said that if you see something beautiful or amazing, you are seeing the work of God. Yeah, well... what did thicky Einstein know... But whether the Universe came to be this way through chance or design is a key question in the science versus religion debate. (More about that on page 19.)

Our Place in the World

General

If you're reading this, then you're almost definitely part of <u>humanity</u>.

Humanity — Homo Sapiens and What Makes Them Special

1) The term <u>humanity</u> can be used in different ways:

It can simply mean all the <u>human beings</u> on the planet — all <u>nearly seven billion</u> of us.

Or it can mean <u>human nature</u>. In particular, all the good ways of acting and feeling that most humans have in common, such as <u>feeling compassion</u>, and <u>doing altruistic (unselfish) deeds</u>.

2) So <u>humanity</u> is kind of what <u>sets us apart</u> from the animals.

3) If you asked a <u>scientist</u> what makes humans special, he or she would be likely to say something about the fact that we're intelligent enough to <u>make and use tools</u>, or that we <u>use language</u> (though it's debatable whether apes do this too — the theories keep changing).

4) But Christians, Jews and Muslims all believe that humans are special because they were <u>created by God in his image</u>, and that humans have <u>two parts</u>, a physical <u>body</u> and a <u>soul</u>.

The soul is the special bit — the bit that lives on after death.

The Big Question — Why Are We Here?

This is a <u>huge question</u> — one that people have been debating for thousands of years.

RELIGIOUS VIEWS

1) Christians believe that we were created by God, <u>for him</u>. Quite simply, he <u>enjoyed creating us</u>, and he likes to <u>love</u> us and have a <u>relationship</u> with each of us.

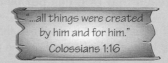
"...all things were created by him and for him."
Colossians 1:16

2) Some verses of the Bible suggest that God created us to look after the rest of his creation. There's lots more on this idea of '<u>stewardship</u>' on the next page.

3) Many Christians, Jews and Muslims believe that what happens <u>after our deaths</u> (see p28-30) depends on how we're judged to have lived. So the purpose of us being here now might be some sort of <u>test</u> — of our morals or faith.

4) Muslims believe that Allah created humans to <u>serve and worship him</u>:

"And I did not create... mankind except to worship Me."
Qur'an 51:56

SCIENTIFIC VIEWS

1) A scientific view is that we're <u>not</u> here for any purpose. No one <u>designed</u> human beings — we're just the products of millions of years of <u>evolution</u> (see the previous page). Like everything else, we're just 'the way things turned out'.

2) It's argued that '<u>special' human characteristics</u>, such as altruism and compassion, are actually things that have evolved to help our genes <u>survive</u> and be passed on to the next generation (e.g. if you help someone in need, they're more likely to help you when you're in need).

3) So human beings are simply another type of animal — they just happen to be a very <u>brainy</u> type.

And the answer is — 42...

Perhaps the entire planet is a huge sort of 'dolls' house' (an extremely complicated one). Or perhaps it's more like an ant farm, where we all scurry about our business, thinking that it's terribly important, while some 'higher being' watches us with amusement. Or maybe we're just minds in glass jars imagining our entire lives...

Environmental Issues

Environmental problems today mean the Earth is suffering. Sadly, many of these problems are __man-made__...

Our Small Planet has some Big Problems

The environmental problems facing the world include...

> Our __environment__ is our __surroundings__ — that we depend on for survival.

i) __Global warming__ (and the __Greenhouse Effect__),
ii) __Deforestation__,
iii) __Extinction__ of animal and plant species,
iv) __Pollution__ (leading to problems like __acid rain__),
v) Scarcity of __natural resources__.

1) __Developed__ countries are the worst (but not the only) polluters. Competition means that businesses often feel forced to put __profit__ before the __welfare__ of the planet — if they don't, they may not survive.
2) Some governments look more to __short-term__ benefits than __long-term__ care for the planet. They may say they're trying to do the best for their __people__, and that __people__ should be our first priority.
3) Governments in __developing nations__ often claim that they're only doing now what richer countries did in the past, and that it's hypocritical for richer countries to tell them what they should be doing.
4) There are things we can __do__, as individuals, to help __minimise__ our impact on the environment. For example, __recycling__ helps conserve natural resources, and walking more, using public transport or using alternative energy resources (e.g. solar power) could reduce __greenhouse gas__ emissions from __fossil fuels__.

Religious Ideas about the Environment — 'Stewardship'

Christianity, Islam and Judaism have pretty similar ideas when it comes to looking after the Earth.
All three religions teach that God has put us in __charge__ of the Earth, but that we must do our duty __responsibly__.

CHRISTIANITY

1) __Christians__ of all denominations believe that God __gave__ us the Earth, but expects us to __care__ for it — this idea is called '__stewardship__'. We have no right to __abuse__ God's creation — we must act __responsibly__.
2) There's pressure on governments and companies to sell goods and services, even at the expense of the environment. Although it can be difficult to balance taking care of the __Earth__ with providing for __humankind__, this is what Christians believe we must __try__ to do.

> "We have a responsibility to create a balanced policy between consumption and conservation." Pope John Paul II, 1988

3) Christianity teaches that everything is __interdependent__ (i.e. everything depends on everything else), so driving species of animal or plant to __extinction__, or harming the __planet__, eventually ends up harming __us__.
4) Christian organisations such as __CAFOD__, __Christian Aid__ (see p17) and __Tearfund®__ are concerned with putting this responsibility into practice. They put pressure on governments and industry to think more about how we are abusing the planet.

> "You made him [humankind] a little lower than the heavenly beings and crowned him with glory and honour. You made him ruler over the works of your hands; you put everything under his feet" Psalm 8:5-6

> "The earth is the Lord's, and everything in it, the world, and all who live in it; for he founded it upon the seas and established it upon the waters." Psalm 24:1-2

> All three religions have organisations that provide opportunities for individuals and communities to use their talents to care for the planet. See p38.

JUDAISM

1) Jews also believe in the concept of __stewardship__. Concern for the natural world is often seen as being at the __heart__ of Jewish teaching.
2) God's creations should remain as he intended, and we have no right to abuse them. Everything is __interdependent__, with trees being seen as particularly important.
3) Jews also believe that as __custodians__, they're responsible for making the world __better__ — this is called _Tikkun Olam_ ('mending the world'). Tikkun Olam isn't __just__ about the environment — it's a general __ideal__ that includes helping the __poor__, and behaving __morally__.

> "The Lord God took the man and put him in the Garden of Eden to work it and take care of it." Genesis 2:15

ISLAM

1) __Muslim__ teaching on environmental issues is very __similar__ to that of Judaism — we are seen as __trustees__ (__khalifah__).
2) At the Day of Judgement we'll have to __answer__ for any ill-treatment of the planet and its resources.
3) The Earth is seen as being a product of the love of Allah, so we should treat it with __love__.

Dr Abdullah Omar Nasseef stated at the 1996 World Wide Fund for Nature conference that, "His [Allah's] trustees are responsible for maintaining the unity of his creation, the integrity of the Earth, its flora and fauna, its wildlife and natural environment."

Look after the planet — or it's eternal damnation for you, my friend...

Again, the ideas of all three of these religions are __very similar__ — we're looking after the place for the 'big man'.

People and Animals

Religions usually say be nice to other people. But what about <u>squirrels</u>...

Christianity says Animals come Below People

According to the Bible, animals were created for the <u>use</u> of mankind — mankind was given <u>dominion</u> (lordship and control) over them. But <u>animal rights</u> issues are still of interest to many Christians. For example...

i) <u>Animal experimentation</u> (e.g. vivisection),
ii) <u>Factory farming</u>,
iii) Destruction of natural <u>habitats</u> (e.g. deforestation), leading to <u>extinction</u>,
iv) <u>Hunting</u>,
v) <u>Genetic modification</u> and <u>cloning</u>,
vi) <u>Zoos</u> and <u>circuses</u>,
vii) <u>Vegetarianism</u>.

1) One of the major issues for Christians is whether animals have <u>souls</u> or not. If they don't, then some people will argue that God created us as <u>superior</u> to them, and that animals are here for our <u>use</u>.

2) Christianity teaches that we should treat animals with <u>kindness</u>, but that they can be used to benefit mankind (as long as their <u>suffering</u> is considered). It's also thought that excessive money should not be 'wasted' on animals when human beings are suffering. So humans are very definitely 'on top', with animals <u>below</u>.

3) But some Christians point out that as everything is <u>interdependent</u>, our treatment of animals reflects on <u>us</u>. Indeed, the Church of England teaches that the medical and technological use of animals should be monitored 'in the light of ethical principles'.

4) The <u>Roman Catholic</u> Church is more likely to tolerate things like <u>animal experimentation</u>, but only if they bring <u>benefit</u> to mankind (e.g. if the experiments lead to the development of life-saving medicines).

5) Certain denominations are generally <u>opposed</u> to any ill-treatment of animals — especially for our pleasure. For example, the <u>Society of Friends</u> (<u>Quakers</u>) are particularly likely to frown upon zoos, animal circuses, hunting and the wearing of fur.

6) Unlike some other religions, there are no specific <u>food laws</u> to be followed in Christianity. So <u>vegetarianism</u> (not eating meat) and <u>veganism</u> (not eating or using any animal products) are a matter for individual Christians to decide about.

"...Rule over the fish of the sea and the birds of the air and over every living creature that moves on the ground." Genesis 1:28

The Bible tells us that Jesus ate <u>fish</u>, and as a Jew he would have eaten <u>meat</u> at certain festivals.

Judaism and Islam have Similar Views

JUDAISM

1) The <u>Noachide Laws</u> (laws given to Noah after the Flood) clearly <u>forbid</u> cruelty to animals. Animals are here to <u>help</u> us, and not to be abused. There are many stories in the Torah that demonstrate <u>care</u> for animals.

2) In Judaism, if meat is to be eaten, the animal must be slaughtered in a 'humane' fashion. This involves cutting the throat of the animal with a very sharp blade to bring about a <u>quick</u> death.

3) <u>Experiments</u> on animals may be tolerated if they result in a benefit for mankind, but only as a last resort. Cruel <u>sports</u> (e.g. bullfighting) are seen as an abuse of God's creatures.

Deuteronomy 5:14 says that animals deserve a day off on the Sabbath, just like people.

"...you shall not do any work, neither you... nor your ox, your donkey or any of your animals..." Deuteronomy 5:14

"...when you slaughter, slaughter in a good way. So every one of you should sharpen his knife, and let the slaughtered animal die comfortably." Prophet Muhammad (Sahih Muslim)

ISLAM

1) <u>Khalifah</u> is the idea that we're responsible for the Earth — khalifah means <u>vice-regent</u>, or <u>trustee</u>.

2) Cruelty to animals is <u>forbidden</u>, as is their use simply for our <u>pleasure</u>.

3) Muslims believe in demonstrating <u>mercy</u> and <u>compassion</u> for all living creatures, and animals used for meat must be slaughtered <u>humanely</u>.

So it's OK to kill them as long as you eat them afterwards...

I bet you thought it would all be simple. You thought I was just going to say something like, 'all religions say be nice to furry things'. Well, they do — to an extent. But this is the page where <u>animal experimentation</u> and stuff comes in, which means <u>benefits for people at the expense of animals</u>. Which complicates things.

Christianity, Judaism, Islam & General

Talents and Caring for the World

Talents aren't just things you show off in front of Simon Cowell — they're any skills that you have.

Talents — It's What We Do With Them That Counts

1) All religions teach that we should serve God to the best of our ability, and most religious people believe that talents are given to us by God — so it's our duty to use them to serve God.

2) Talents can be anything — pretty much everyone has something useful they can do. For example, good singers could use their talent to worship God in the church choir, good bakers could make cakes to sell to raise money for religious projects, good public speakers could preach religious messages...

3) There are plenty of other ways to use talents too, e.g. if you're patient, maybe you could care for the sick, or if your skills are more practical, perhaps you could use them to improve the environment (see below).

4) The Parable of the Talents (Matthew 25:14-30) explains the Christian attitude to talents:

A man was going away, and entrusted some money to each of his three servants. To the first he gave five talents, to the second he gave two talents, and to the third he gave one talent.

You twit.

The first two servants used their talents wisely, and doubled them. When their master came home, he was pleased with them both.

The third servant had simply buried his talent, for safe-keeping. The master was very angry with him, took the talent off him, and threw him out.

The 'talents' in this parable are actually units of currency. But it's been interpreted as talking about any of God's gifts, such as our inborn skills. In fact, this is thought to be where our word 'talent' comes from.

It doesn't matter how many talents you have, it's what you do with them that counts.

It's when you don't even try that God gets angry.

5) Many non-religious people believe it's good to develop and use your talents. It'll give you more satisfaction in life, and with any luck, you'll make the world a better place along the way.

You Can Use Your Talents to Care for the Environment

There are lots of organisations that'll help you use your talents to take care of the planet. They won't make you plant trees if you're the type that cries if you break a nail — they'll find something that your talents will suit.

Here are some examples of religious organisations that provide opportunities for individuals and communities to use their talents to care for the planet...

Faiths4Change is an organisation in the North West of England that helps people from all faith communities to improve their local environments. For example, they run projects that help children to grow vegetables in their school grounds.

A Rocha is a Christian environment and conservation movement. They encourage individuals to help in all sorts of ways — from collecting data on endangered bumblebees, to using cycling as a 'green' way of getting about. Church groups are given ideas to help them improve the eco-friendliness of church buildings and grounds, and other communities are encouraged to work together to improve their local area, e.g. by turning derelict wasteland into nature gardens. A Rocha also provides church resources for environment-themed services.

The Noah Project raises awareness of environmental issues throughout the Jewish community, through education and practical action. They also produce environment-based resources for use at Jewish festivals.

The activities of The Islamic Foundation for Ecology and Environmental Sciences (IFEES) range from waging 'eco-jihad' in Birmingham by picking up litter, to building a new environmentally friendly village for refugees and tsunami survivors in Indonesia.

So plant trees, not talents (or small children)...

The main point is that religions teach that God created the world so we should look after it. And we can do this best by using our talents. Being an eco-warrior isn't the only way to use your talents though — there are plenty of ways to do good with them. And even if you're non-religious, it'll still give you a warm glow inside.

Practice Questions

*Makes you think doesn't it... How did life begin? What's the point to it all?
Should I have a bacon or cheese sandwich for lunch?*

You need to have your own views on this stuff, but you won't get far in the exam if you don't know some religious teachings as well. So try these questions, and if there are any you can't answer, go back and have another look at the section. Then try the questions again until you can do them all.

1) Explain what religious believers mean by:

   a) creation.

   b) dominion.

   c) humanity.

   d) soul.

   e) stewardship.

   f) talents.

   g) khalifah. *(Islam)*

   h) Tikkun Olam. *(Judaism)*

These are worth only 2 marks each. So get straight to the point — don't write an essay.

2) Explain how having a religious faith might support the view that:

   a) humans are special.

   b) we should try not to use up more natural resources than we need to.

   c) animal experimentation is not wrong.

   d) we should put our talents to good use.

Don't forget — use religious terms correctly in these 4-markers. "Stewardship" and "dominion" are good ones to get in here.

3) Give <u>two</u> reasons why a religious believer might agree or disagree with each of these statements:

   a) "God created the Universe and everything in it in six days."

   b) "Humans should use the environment for their benefit."

   c) "Eating meat is not wrong."

Make sure you include religious teachings here — if you can quote a bit of scripture, so much the better. These questions are worth 4 marks each.

4) Explain, from <u>two</u> different religious traditions:

   a) beliefs about creation.

   b) beliefs about our relationship with animals.

   c) how individuals and communities are using their talents to care for the environment.

These questions are worth 6 marks each, so you have to give <u>detailed</u> answers.

5) Say whether you agree with each of these statements.
Give reasons for your answer, showing that you have thought of more than one point of view. You must refer to religious beliefs.

   a) "We were not put here for any purpose. Humans just evolved by chance."

   b) "Religious and scientific beliefs about creation can't both be true."

   c) "Religious people are more likely to treat animals well."

These 8-mark questions can make a big difference to your grade. Have a look at p41 for some advice on answering them.

General

Do Well in Your Exam

You've learnt all the <u>facts</u> — now it's time to get those <u>grades</u>.

You'll have a 1¾ Hour Exam on Religion and Life Issues

1) For the <u>Religion and Life Issues</u> exam you'll have to answer four questions, with one on each topic — <u>Relationships</u>, <u>Is it Fair?</u>, <u>Looking for Meaning</u>, and <u>Our World</u>.

2) Each question will come with its own selection of '<u>visual stimuli</u>' — <u>pictures</u> and bits of <u>writing</u> that might help with answering the questions.

3) Each question will come in <u>five parts</u>, labelled (a) to (e).

You Get Marks for What You Know and How You Express It

In GCSE Religious Studies there are two <u>Assessment Objectives</u>:

You get <u>half</u> your marks for <u>describing</u> and <u>explaining</u> what you <u>know</u>, and the rest for using <u>arguments</u> and <u>evidence</u> to <u>explain</u> and <u>evaluate</u> what you and others think.

From January 2013, 5% of the marks in RS exams will be for spelling, punctuation and grammar. Make sure that your writing is as accurate as possible.

There are Easy Marks for Knowing What Things Mean

Part (<u>a</u>) of each question asks you to define what an <u>important concept</u> means to <u>religious believers</u>. These questions are only worth <u>2 marks</u> so keep your answer fairly <u>short</u> and <u>to the point</u> — but make sure you define and explain the word <u>properly</u>. Learn the details of the key terms in the <u>glossary</u> (p42-43).

a) Explain what religious believers mean by 'afterlife'. (2 marks)

The term 'afterlife' means that existence religious people believe they will move on to after their physical death.

Make your answer as clear as possible.

You Have to Explain the Impact of Faith on People's Lives

Part (<u>b</u>) of each question is worth <u>4 marks</u>, which you'll get for <u>explaining</u> or describing how <u>religious beliefs</u> might <u>influence</u> a person's <u>actions</u>, <u>views</u> and <u>practices</u>.

b) Explain how having a religious faith might encourage a person to get married. (4 marks)

Many religious traditions place great importance on <u>having children</u>.
They also teach that marriage is the best foundation to start a family.
Muslims believe that the <u>sexual impulse</u> is powerful, and that the right context for a sexual relationship is in a marriage. Religions usually frown on <u>cohabitation</u>.

Include some of the specialist language you've learnt.

There are Reasons for what Believers think

For part (<u>c</u>) you'll be given a <u>statement</u>, and asked to give <u>two</u> reasons why a religious believer might or might not agree with it. This question carries <u>4 marks</u>.

c) 'Science has shown that accounts of creation in the scriptures are wrong. This means the rest of the scriptures may be wrong.'
Give **two** reasons why a religious believer might agree or disagree with this statement. (4 marks)

(i) Some religious people believe that the creation story was an early attempt to explain how the world came into being. Even though this has been superseded by scientific knowledge, their faith is based on the <u>moral teachings</u> in their scriptures, rather than theories about the beginning of the universe.

(ii) Other believers may feel that although creation stories should no longer be accepted as literal truth, they can be interpreted <u>symbolically</u>. They were intended to tells us about the <u>goodness of creation</u>, and how <u>humanity is the creation of God</u>.

Try to give two well developed answers with explanations or examples of what you mean.

Do Well in Your Exam

More stuff for you on the <u>exam</u> right here. Get <u>stuck in</u>.

Learn What Religious People Do and Why

For part (<u>d</u>) you'll be asked to explain some aspect of <u>religious teaching</u> or <u>practice</u> for <u>two religious traditions</u>. These can be two different religions, e.g. Christianity and Islam, or two different Christian traditions, e.g. Protestantism and Roman Catholicism. It's really important in these longer-answer questions that you write in <u>good</u>, <u>clear English</u>, and that you use <u>technical terms</u> properly.

> d) Explain how symbolism is used in **two** different religious traditions.
> (You must state the religious traditions you are referring to.) (6 marks)

Remember — all Christian traditions are not the same. Say which ones you're referring too.

You need to explain the impact of people's beliefs on their actions.

(i) The most common <u>Christian</u> symbol is the <u>cross</u>. It reminds believers of the <u>resurrection</u>. Christians will often put a <u>fish symbol</u> on the back of their cars to demonstrate their faith to others.

In Orthodox Christianity, churches are filled with <u>icons</u> that represent Jesus, Mary, the angels and the saints. Worshippers kiss the images, which they believe brings the presence of those who they represent into the church.

(ii) In <u>Islam</u>, images of Muhammad or Allah are not allowed. This is because such images are seen as creating the temptation to commit idolatry. For this reason Arabic characters are used to represent them. All mosques have a <u>dome</u> to symbolise the universe. <u>Green</u> is a commonly used colour in Islam as it was believed to be Muhammad's favourite colour and represents life.

You'll Have to Give Your Opinion — And Back It Up

For part (<u>e</u>) you'll be given a <u>statement</u> and asked whether you <u>agree</u> with it or not. But what you'll really get the marks for is how you back up your answer with <u>reasons</u>. You have to make reference to <u>religious beliefs</u>, and you'll need to show that you understand <u>both sides</u> of the argument.

They <u>don't</u> tell you in the question (so I reckon it's a bit sneaky) — to get <u>top marks</u> you have to include reasoning from at least <u>two different</u> religious traditions, and <u>moral</u> reasoning, in your answer.

> e) 'A religious person should have no more wealth than they need to live.'
> Do you agree? Give reasons or evidence for your answer, showing that you have thought of more than one point of view. You must include reference to religious beliefs in your answer. (8 marks)

It doesn't hurt if you can remember some scripture.

Think about the impact holding your views would have on society.

You need to show that you've thought about other viewpoints.

I agree with this statement, because religions teach the importance of charity, and helping others. In Luke it says that "The man with two tunics should share with him that has none..." This shows that if Christians have more than they need they should use it to help the poor.

Judaism goes even further. All Jews, however rich or poor they are, are expected to use a portion of their wealth to help the poor. But Judaism also teaches that poverty will make others responsible for you, so you shouldn't shun wealth.

Jesus says in the book of Matthew that it is "easier for a camel to go through the eye of a needle than for a rich man to enter the kingdom of God." Although he states that God makes all things possible, it still seems to suggest that for the truly religious, being wealthy is not recommended.

But many Christians would argue that it is focusing on wealth and material things that is the problem, rather than the actual fact of being wealthy. For this they could argue that the Bible says that it is the "love of money that is the root of all evil" and that money itself is not a problem.

Thou shalt use specialist language...

Even if you know every little fact in this book, a large chunk of how well you do in the exam will come down to, well... how good you are at exams. Make sure you spend enough time reading through these pages, and enough time practising the exam-style questions at the end of each Topic. It'll all pay off in the end, I promise.

Glossary

Everyone needs the blue definitions. The green ones are for Islam only. The purple ones are for Judaism only.

adultery	A married person having sex with someone who isn't their husband or wife. It can also be used more generally to mean cheating on your partner, whether you're married or not.
afterlife	The belief that some sort of life continues after death, and the form that life takes.
authority	Something that influences or controls you, e.g. the law or religious teachings.
awe	A feeling of deep respect mixed with fear.
celibacy	Never getting married or having sex.
charismatic phenomena	Experiences in which Christian worshippers feel they have been 'touched by the Holy Spirit'. These range from dancing, shaking and crying to 'speaking in tongues' (unknown languages).
chastity	Not having sex — remaining a virgin.
cohabitation	Living together in a sexual relationship without being married.
commitment	A promise to do something. Keeping the promise will mean that you aren't totally free.
community	A group of people who live together, or have something in common, e.g. religion or race.
conflict	A serious disagreement or difference of opinion.
contraception	Anything that aims to prevent a woman becoming pregnant.
courtship	A period of 'dating', where two people are romantically involved before marriage.
creation	The act of making something, or the thing that has been made. In Religious Studies, this usually refers to the creation of the Universe by God/Allah.
discrimination	Treating different people, or groups of people, differently (usually unfairly).
dominion	'Lordship' of and control over something. In Genesis, humans were given dominion over the animals — the animal were given to humans to use.
environment	Our surroundings, which we (and all other animals and plants) depend on for survival.
equality	Everyone being treated equally, and considered to be just as important as everyone else.
First Cause	The starting point of the Universe — the uncaused cause. This is often used as a title for God.
free will	The ability to choose how to behave. All three religions believe humans have free will.
Gemilut Hasadim	Kind and compassionate actions towards those in need.
God	A god is a divine being who is the subject of reverence or worship for a religion. With a capital 'G', God usually refers to the all-powerful, all-knowing Judeo-Christian god.
human dignity	The idea that all human life is valuable and everyone has the right to be treated with respect.
humanity	Either the human race or the caring nature of humans towards each other.
identity	All the characteristics that make you who you are.
immanent	An immanent god is a god who is in the world with us and takes an active role in our lives.
injustice	Unfairness. Not treating someone as they have a right to be treated.
ketubah	The marriage contract, which sets out a Jewish couple's rights and responsibilities.
khalifah	The idea that Muslims are responsible for the environment as Allah's 'trustees' or 'vice-regents'.
kiddushin	Betrothal — the first part of the Jewish marriage ceremony.
love	Immense and unconditional kindness and affection.

Glossary

mahr	A dowry paid by a groom to the bride when they get married.
miracle	An event usually believed to be the work of God, that can't be explained by the laws of science.
mourning	A deep sorrow for someone who has died. During a period of mourning, loved ones usually pray for the deceased and go without pleasures (e.g. music, bright colours, sex).
nikah	The marriage contract drawn up by the family of the bride and groom.
numinous	An experience that inspires awe and wonder, in which someone can feel God's presence.
omni-benevolent	Showing unlimited love and compassion.
omnipotent	Having unlimited power — all things are possible.
omniscient	Knowing everything — in the past, present and future.
prejudice	Judging something or someone with no good reason, or without full knowledge of a situation.
promiscuity	Having many sexual partners.
racism	Discrimination against people of other races — often based on unfair stereotypes.
reconciliation	Returning to harmony and friendship after conflict.
responsibility	Having to answer for your own actions. A responsibility is also a duty to do something or care for someone.
revelation	An experience that reveals God's presence to someone.
secular society	A society in which government and religion are kept completely separate.
Sadaqah	Aid given by Muslims in addition to the compulsory Zakah, e.g. money or an act of compassion.
sex discrimination	Treating someone unfairly based on their gender (male or female).
Shari'ah	The Islamic law code — it lays out rules for day-to-day living. It's based on the Qur'an, the Hadith (sayings) and Sunnah (lifestyle) of Muhammad, and the customs of the Muslim community.
social justice	Treating everyone as they deserve, so that all their basic needs are met and their rights are respected — whatever their race, religion or social class.
social responsibility	Considering the effect that our actions have on other people.
soul	The spiritual part of a human. It is separate from the body and is the part that many people believe lives on after death.
stewardship	The idea that God gave humans the Earth, but expects them to take care of it.
symbolism	Images, objects or actions that represent religious ideas, e.g. the dove represents peace.
talents	Skills that you have or things that you can do well. Christians, Jews and Muslims believe that talents are gifts from God/Allah.
Tawhid	The Muslim belief in the oneness and incomparability of Allah.
Tikkun Olam	The Jewish concept of 'mending the world'.
Tzedakah	The Jewish practice of giving 10% of their wealth to the poor.
vocation	Something that you are 'called to' do by God — your special mission in life.
worship	Any way in which a religious believer expresses their love for, and devotion to, a god.
Zakah	A Pillar of Islam — Muslims must donate 2.5% of their yearly savings to the poor.

Index